JUSTIFICATION BY FAITH

Paul's Letter to the Christians at Rome

by

William MacDonald

WALTERICK PUBLISHERS
P.O. Box 2216
Kansas City, Kansas 66110

Except where otherwise indicated, all Scripture quotations in this book are taken from the King James Version of the Bible (abbreviated KJV).

Verses marked NASB are taken from The New American Standard Bible, © The Lockman Foundation 1960, 1962, 1963, 1968, 1971, 1972, 1973, 1975. Used by permission.

Other Bible versions (and abbreviations) are listed in the Bibliography at the back of this book

JUSTIFICATION BY FAITH

Copyright © 1981 by William MacDonald

Published by Walterick Publishers
Kansas City, Kansas 66110

ISBN 0-937396-36-2

CONTENTS

The Epistle To The Romans
INTRODUCTION

How did Christianity first reach Rome? We can't be positive, but it may be that Jews from Rome who were converted in Jerusalem on the Day of Pentecost (see Acts 2:10) carried back the good news. That was in A.D. 30.

Paul had never been in Rome when he wrote this letter from Corinth 28 years later. But he knew quite a few of the Christians there, as is seen in chapter 16. Christians in those days were people on the move, whether as a result of persecution or as heralds of the gospel or in the ordinary course of their work. These Christians in Rome were from both Jewish and Gentile backgrounds.

Paul finally did reach Rome around A.D. 60, but not in the way he expected. He came as a prisoner of Christ Jesus.

His Letter to the Romans is a classic. The unsaved can go to it for a clear exposition of their sinful, lost condition and of God's righteous plan for saving them. Young believers learn of their identification with Christ and of victory through the power of the Holy Spirit. Mature believers find never-ending delight in its wide spectrum of Christian truth—doctrinal, prophetical, and practical. In order to see for ourselves why it is such a beloved letter, let us turn to chapter 1.

CHAPTER 1

The best way to understand the Epistle to the Romans is to see it as a dialogue between Paul and some unnamed objector. As Paul sets forth the doctrine of the gospel, he seems to hear this objector raising all kinds of arguments against it. The apostle patiently replies to his opponent's questions one by one. By the time he is finished, Paul has answered every major attitude that the mind of man can take regarding the gospel of the grace of God.

Sometimes the objections are clearly stated, and sometimes they are only implied. But whether stated or implied, they all revolve around the gospel—the good news of salvation by grace through faith in the Lord Jesus Christ, apart from the works of the law.

We will think of the Letter to the Romans as dealing with 11 main questions, as follows:

1. What is the subject of the letter? (1:1,9,15,16)
2. What is the gospel? (1:1-17)
3. Why do men need the gospel? (1:18—3:20)
4. According to the gospel, how can ungodly sinners be justified by a holy God? (3:21-31)
5. Does the gospel agree with the teachings of the Old Testament Scripture? (4:1-25)
6. What are the benefits of justification in the believer's life? (5:1-21)
7. Does the teaching of the gospel (salvation by grace through faith) encourage or even permit sinful living? (6:1-23)

7

8. What is the relationship of the Christian to the law? (7:1-25)
9. How is the Christian enabled to live a holy life? (8:1-39)
10. Does the gospel, by promising salvation to Gentiles as well as Jews, mean that God has broken His promises to His earthly people, the Jews? (9:1—11:36)
11. How should those who have been justified by grace respond in their everyday lives? (12:1—16:27)

If you acquaint yourself with these 11 questions and learn the answers to them, you will have at least a working knowledge of this important epistle.

The first question is:

What is the subject of the letter?

The answer, of course, is "the gospel." Paul wastes no time in getting to the point. Four times in the first 16 verses he mentions it (vv. 1,9,15,16).

But then the question arises:

What is the gospel?

The word itself means *good news*. But in verses 1-17 the apostle tells us six important facts about the good news.

As to its source, it is the gospel of God (v. 1).

As to its relation to the Old Testament, it was promised by the prophetic Scriptures (v. 2).

As to its content, it is good news concerning God's Son, the Lord Jesus Christ (v. 3).

As to its effectiveness, it is God's power unto salvation (v. 16).

As to its availability, it is for all men, Gentiles as well as Jews (v. 16).

As to its terms, it is by faith alone (v. 17).

With that as an introduction, let us now go back and take up these verses one by one.

1:1 In this first verse, Paul introduces himself as one who was:

purchased—this is implied in the designation "a bondslave of Jesus Christ";

called—on the road to Damascus he was called to be an apostle—that is, a special emissary of the Savior;

separated—that is, he was set apart to take the good news of God to the Gentiles (see Acts 9:15; 13:2).

We too have been purchased by the precious blood of Christ, called to be witnesses to His saving power, and set apart to tell the good news wherever we go.

1:2 Lest any of Paul's Jewish readers might think that the gospel is completely new and unrelated to their spiritual heritage, the apostle mentions that the Old Testament prophets had promised it. They had promised it in clear-cut statements (Deuteronomy 18:15; Isaiah 7:14; Habakkuk 2:4) and in types and symbols (for example, Noah's ark, the serpent of brass, and the sacrificial system).

1:3 The gospel is the good news concerning God's Son, the Lord Jesus Christ, who is a lineal descendant of David according to the flesh (that is, as far as His humanity is concerned). In using the expression *according to the flesh,* Paul implies that our Lord is more than a man. The words mean *as to His humanity.* If Christ were only a man, it would be unnecessary to single out this feature of His being, since there would be no other. But He is more than man, as Paul goes on to show in the next verse.

1:4 The Lord Jesus is marked out as the Son of God in power. The Holy Spirit, who is here called the Spirit of holiness, marked Jesus out at His baptism and throughout His miracle-working ministry. The Savior's mighty miracles, performed in the power of the Holy Spirit, bore witness to the fact that He is the Son of God.* When we read that He is "declared to be the Son of God with power . . . by the resurrection from the dead," we naturally think of His own resurrection. But the literal reading here is "by resurrection of dead persons," and so the apostle may also be

---

*Some commentators understand the expression "the spirit of holiness" to refer to Christ's own holy being—that is, to His own human spirit.

thinking of Christ's raising of Jairus' daughter, of the widow of Nain's son, and of Lazarus. However, there is little question that it is the Lord's own resurrection that is primarily in view.

When we say that Jesus is God's Son, we mean that He is a Son like no one else is. God has many sons. All believers are His sons (Galatians 4:5-7). Even angels are spoken of as sons (Job 1:6; 2:1). But Jesus is God's Son in a *unique* sense. When our Lord spoke of God as His Father, the Jews rightly understood Him to be claiming equality with God (John 5:18).

1:5 It was through Jesus Christ our Lord that Paul received grace and apostleship. The same undeserved favor that saved him also entrusted him with apostleship. Paul was commissioned to call men of all nations to obedience of faith—that is, to obey the message of the gospel by repenting of their sins and believing on the Lord Jesus Christ (Acts 20:21). And the goal of this world-wide proclamation of the message was for "His Name's sake," which simply means to please Him and to bring glory to Him. When Paul says "*we* have received grace and apostleship," he is almost certainly using the editorial *we,* referring to himself alone. The way he links apostleship with the nations or Gentiles points to him and not to the other apostles.

1:6 Among those who had responded to the gospel call were those to whom Paul wrote, and whom he dignifies with the title "called to be Jesus Christ's" (ASV). This title emphasizes the godward side of salvation. It was God who took the initiative.

1:7 The letter is addressed to all believers in Rome, and not (as in other epistles) to a single assembly. It appears from the final chapter of the letter that there were several gatherings of believers in the city, and this salutation embraces them all.

"Beloved of God, called saints." These two lovely names are true of all who have been redeemed by the precious blood of Christ. These favored ones are objects of divine love in a special way, and they are also called to be set apart to God from the world, for that is the meaning of *saints.*

Paul's characteristic greeting combines grace and peace. Grace *(charis)* is the usual Greek salutation, and peace *(shalom)* is the Jewish greeting. The combination is especially appropriate because Paul's message tells how believing Jews and Gentiles are now one new man in Christ.

The grace mentioned here is not the grace that saves (since Paul's readers were already saved) but the grace that equips and empowers for Christian life and service. And the peace is not so much peace with God (the saints already had that because they were justified by faith) but rather the peace of God reigning in their hearts while they were in the midst of a turbulent society.

Notice that grace and peace come from God the Father and the Lord Jesus Christ. This strongly implies the equality of the Son with the Father. If Jesus were no more than a man, it would be absurd to list Him as equal with the Father in bestowing grace and peace. It would be like saying, "Grace and peace from God the Father and from Abraham Lincoln."

1:8 Whenever possible, the apostle began his letters by expressing appreciation for whatever was commendable in his readers. (A good example for all of us!) Here he thanks God through Jesus Christ, the Mediator, that the faith of the Roman Christians was proclaimed throughout the whole world. Their testimony as Christians was talked about throughout the whole Roman Empire, which then constituted the "whole world" from the perspective of those living in the Mediterranean area.

1:9 Because they let their light so shine before men, Paul was constrained to pray for them unceasingly. He calls God as his witness to the constancy of his prayers, because no one else could know this. But God knows—the God whom the apostle served in his spirit in the gospel of His Son.

Paul's service was in his spirit. It was not that of a religious drudge, going through endless rituals and reciting prayers and liturgies by rote. It was service that was bathed in fervent, believing prayers. It was willing, devoted, tireless service, fired by a spirit that loved the Lord Jesus supremely. It was a flaming passion to make known the good news about God's Son. It was the kind of service which F.W.H. Myers captured in these lines from his memorable poem *St. Paul:*

Only like souls I see the folk thereunder,
Bound who should conquer, slaves who should be
    kings,
Hearing their one hope with an empty wonder,
Sadly contented with a show of things.

Then with a rush the intolerable craving
Shivers throughout me like a trumpet call.
O to save these, to perish for their saving,
Die for their life, be offered for them all![1]

1:10 Coupled with Paul's thanksgiving to God for the Roman saints was his continual prayer that he might visit them in the not-too-distant future. As with everything else he did, he wanted his journey to be according to God's will.

1:11 The impelling desire of the apostle's heart was to help the saints along spiritually so that they might be further established in the faith. There is no thought here of his conferring some "second blessing" on them, as the term is used today. Neither did he intend to impart some spiritual gift by the laying on of his hands (though he did this in the case of Timothy, as we learn in 2 Timothy 1:6). It was entirely a matter of helping their spiritual growth through the ministry of the Word.

1:12 He goes on to explain that there would actually be mutual blessing. He would be encouraged by their faith, and they by his. In all edifying intercourse, there is spiritual enrichment. "Iron sharpens iron, so one man sharpens another" (Proverbs 27:17 NASB). Note Paul's humility and graciousness—he was not above being helped by other saints.

1:13 He had often desired to visit Rome but had been prevented, perhaps by the pressing needs in other areas, perhaps by the direct restraint of the Holy Spirit, perhaps by the opposition of Satan. He desired to have fruit among the Gentiles in Rome as he had among people of other nations. Here he is speaking of fruit in the gospel, as the next two verses indicate. In verses 11 and 12 his aim was to see the Roman Christians built up in their faith. Here he desires to see souls won for Christ in the capital of the Roman Empire.

1:14 Anyone who has Christ has the answer to the world's deepest need. He has the cure to the disease of sin, the way to escape the eternal horrors of hell, and the guarantee of everlasting happiness with God. This puts him under solemn obligation to share the good news with men of all cultures—Greeks and foreigners—and men of all degrees of learning—wise and unwise. Paul felt the obligation keenly. He said "I am debtor . . ."

1:15 To discharge that debt, he was ready to preach the gospel in Rome with all the power God gave him. It was surely not to the believers in Rome, as this verse might seem to suggest, for they had already responded to the glad tidings. But he was ready to preach to the unconverted Gentiles there in the metropolis.

1:16 "I am debtor," "I am ready," and now "I am not ashamed." Paul was not ashamed to take God's good news to sophisticated Rome, even though the message had proved to be a stumbling block to the Jews and foolishness to the Greeks. For he knew that it is the power of God unto salvation—that is, it tells how God by His mighty power saves everyone who believes on His Son. And this power is extended equally to Jews and Greeks.

The order "to the Jew first and also to the Greek" was fulfilled historically during the Acts period. While we still have an enduring obligation to God's ancient people, the Jews, we are not required to evangelize them before going to the Gentiles. Today God deals with Jews and Gentiles on the same basis, and the message and timing are the same to all.

1:17 Since the word "righteousness" occurs here for the first time in the letter, we will pause to consider its meaning. Actually the word is used in several different ways in the New Testament, but we shall consider only three uses.

First of all, it is used to describe that characteristic of God by which He always does that which is right, just, proper, and consistent with all His other attributes. When we say that God is righteous, we mean that there is no wrong, dishonesty, or unfairness in Him.

Then, secondly, the righteousness of God can refer to His method of justifying ungodly sinners. He can do this and still be righteous because Jesus as the sinless Substitute has satisfied all the claims of divine justice.

Finally, the righteousness of God refers to the perfect standing which God provides for those who believe on His Son (2 Corinthians 5:21). Those who are not in themselves righteous are treated as if they were righteous because God sees them in all the perfection of Christ. Righteousness is imputed to their account.

Which is the meaning here in verse 17? While it could be any of the three, the righteousness of God seems to refer especially to His way of justifying sinners by faith.

The righteousness of God is revealed in the gospel. First the gospel tells us that God's inflexible righteousness demands that sins be punished, and the penalty is eternal death. But then we hear that God's love provided what His righteousness demanded. He sent His Son to die as a Substitute for sinners, paying the penalty in full. Now because His righteous claims have been fully satisfied, God can righteously save all those who avail themselves of the work of Christ.

God's righteousness is revealed from faith to faith. The expression ''from faith to faith'' seems to mean ''by faith from first to last'' (NIV). God's righteousness is not imputed on the basis of works or made available to those who seek to earn or deserve it. It is revealed on the principle of faith alone.

This is in perfect agreement with the divine decree in Habakkuk 2:4, ''The just shall live by faith,'' which may also be understood to mean ''The justified-by-faith-ones shall live.''

In the first 17 verses of Romans, Paul has introduced his subject and has stated very briefly some of the principal points, which he will explain in greater detail as he proceeds.

This brings us to the third main question: *Why do men need the gospel* (1:18—3:20)?

The answer, in brief, is because they are lost without it. But this raises four subsidiary questions.

Are the heathen who have never heard the gospel lost (1:18-32)?

Are the self-righteous moralists, whether Jews or Gentiles, lost (2:1-16)?

Are God's ancient earthly people, the Jews, lost (2:17–3:8)?

Are all men lost (3:9-20)?

1:18 Here we have the answer to the question *Why do men need the gospel?* The answer is that they are lost without it, and that God's wrath is revealed from heaven against the wickedness of men who suppress the truth in unrighteousness. But how is God's wrath revealed? One answer is given in the context. God gives men over to uncleanness (1:24), to vile affections (1:26), and to a reprobate mind (1:28). But it is also true that God occasionally breaks through into human history to show His extreme displeasure at man's sin—for example, the flood (Genesis 7); the destruction of Sodom and Gomorrah (Genesis 19); and the punishment of Korah, Dathan, and Abiram (Numbers 16:32).

1:19 *Are the heathen lost who have never heard?* The apostle shows that they are, not because of the knowledge they don't have, but because of the light which they do have and yet refuse!

Those things which may be known of God in creation have been revealed to them. God has not left them without a revelation of Himself.

1:20 Ever since the creation of the world, two invisible characteristics of God have been on display for all to see—namely, His eternal power and His divinity or godhood.The word Paul uses here is better translated *divinity* or *godhood* (rather than *godhead*, as in the KJV). It means the character of God rather than His essential being, His glorious attributes rather than His inherent deity. His deity is assumed.

The argument here is clear: Creation demands a Creator. Design demands a Designer. By looking up at the sun, moon, and stars, any man can know that there is a God.

So the answer to the question "What about the heathen?" is this: they are without excuse. God has revealed Himself to them in creation, but they have not responded to this revelation. They have not trusted the one true God. They have not worshiped Him. So "men are not condemned for rejecting a Savior they have never heard of, but for not being faithful to what they could know of God."[2]

1:21 Though they knew God by His works, they did not glorify Him for who He is or thank Him for all He has done. Rather, they gave themselves over to foolish, empty philosophies and speculations about other gods, and as a result they lost the capacity to see and think clearly. "Light rejected is light denied." Those who don't want to see lose the capacity to see.

1:22 As men grew more conceited over their self-styled knowledge, they plunged deeper into ignorance and nonsense. These two things always characterize those who reject the knowledge of God—they become insufferably conceited and abysmally ignorant at the same time.

1:23 Instead of evolving from lower forms, early man was of a high moral order. By refusing to acknowledge the true, infinite, incorruptible God, he *de*volved to the stupidity and depravity that go with idol worship. This whole passage gives the lie to evolution.

Man is instinctively a religious creature. He must have some object to worship. When he refused to worship the living God, he made his own gods by carving corruptible images of wood and stone representing men, birds, animals, and reptiles.

Notice the downward progression—men, birds, animals, and reptiles. And remember that man becomes like what he worships. As his concept of god degenerates, his morals degenerate also. If his god is a reptile, then he feels free to live as he pleases.

Remember too that a worshiper generally considers himself inferior to the object of his worship. Created in the image and after the likeness of God, man here takes a place lower than that of serpents!

And never forget that when man worships idols, he worships demons. Paul states clearly that the things which the Gentiles sacrifice to idols they sacrifice to demons and not to God (1 Corinthians 10:20).

1:24 Three times it is said that God gave man up. He gave them up to uncleanness (1:24), to vile passions (1:26), and to a reprobate mind (1:28). In other words, God's wrath was directed against man's entire personality.

In response to the evil lusts of their hearts, God abandoned them to heterosexual uncleanness—adultery, fornication, lasciviousness, prostitution, harlotry, etc. Life became for them a round of sex orgies in which they dishonored their bodies among themselves.

1:25 This abandonment by God was because they first abandoned the truth about Him for the lie of idolatry. An idol is a lie, a false representation of God, a caricature of the truth. An idolater worships the image of a creature—whether man, bird, beast, or snake—and thus insults and dishonors the Creator, who is eternally worthy of honor and glory, not of insult.

1:26 For this same reason God gave people over to erotic activity with members of their own sex. Women became lesbians, practicing unnatural sex and knowing no shame.

1:27 Men became sodomites, in total perversion of their natural functions. Turning away from the marriage relationship ordained by God, they burned with lust for other men and became practicing homosexuals.

But their sin took its toll in their own bodies and souls. Disease, guilt, and personality deformities struck at them like the sting of a scorpion. This disproves the notion that anyone can commit this sin and get away with it.

Homosexuality is being passed off today by some as a sickness and by others as a legitimate alternative lifestyle. Christians must be careful not to accept the world's moral judgments but to be guided by God's Word. In the Old Testament this sin was punishable by death (Leviticus 18:29; 20:13), and here in the New Testament those who practice it are said to be worthy of death (Romans 1:32). The Bible speaks of homosexuality as sin of a very serious nature as evidenced by God's obliteration of Sodom and Gomorrah, where gay militants ran riot (Genesis 19:4-25).

The gospel offers pardon and forgiveness to homosexuals, as

to all sinners who repent and believe in the Lord Jesus Christ. Christians who have fallen into this heinous sin can find forgiveness and restoration through confessing and forsaking the sin. There is complete and final deliverance from homosexuality to all who are willing to obey God's Word. Ongoing counseling assistance is very important in every case.

It is true that some people seem to have a natural tendency toward homosexuality. This should not be surprising, since fallen human nature is capable of just about any form of iniquity and perversion. The gross sin is not in the inclination toward it but in yielding to it and practicing it. The Holy Spirit gives the power to resist the temptation and to have lasting victory (1 Corinthians 10:13). Some of the Christians in Corinth were living proofs that homosexuals need not be irrevocably bound to that lifestyle (1 Corinthians 6:9-11).

1:28 Because of men's refusal to retain God in their knowledge, either as Creator, Sustainer, or Deliverer, God gave them up to a depraved mind to commit a catalog of other forms of wickedness. This verse gives deep insight into why evolution has such enormous appeal for natural men. The reason does not lie in their intellects but in their wills. They do not want to retain God in their knowledge. It is not that the evidence for evolution is so overwhelming that they are compelled to accept it; rather, it is because they want some explanation for origins that will eliminate God completely.

1:29 Here, then, is the dark list of additional sins which characterize man in his alienation from God. And notice that he is *full* of them; he is not just an occasional dabbler in them. He is trained in sins that are not fitting for a human being.

unrighteousness—injustice.

fornication (KJV)—omitted in later versions. This sin was probably covered in verse 24.

wickedness—destructiveness.

covetousness—greed, avarice, the incessant desire for more, whether material or sexual.

maliciousness—the deep-seated desire for harm on others; venomous hatred.

full of envy—jealousy of others because of what they are or have.

full of murder—premeditated and unlawful killing of another, either in anger or in the commission of some other crime.

full of debate—strife, wrangling, quarreling, contentiousness.

full of deceit—guile, trickery, treachery, intrigue.

full of malignity—ill-will, spite, hostility, bitterness.

whisperers—secret slanderers, gossips.

1:30 *backbiters*—open slanderers, those who bad-mouth others.

haters of God—or hateful to God.

insolent—despiteful, insulting.

proud—haughty, arrogant.

boastful—bragging, vaunting oneself.

inventors of evil things—devisers of mischief and new forms of wickedness.

disobedient to parents—rebellious at parental authority.

1:31 *without understanding*—lacking moral and spiritual discernment, without conscience.

covenant-breakers—breaking promises, treaties, agreements, and contracts whenever it serves their purposes.

without natural affection—acting in total disregard of natural ties and the obligations that go with them.

implacable (KJV)—omitted in the best and most ancient manuscripts.

unmerciful—cruel, vindictive, heartless, without pity.

1:32 Those who abuse sex (1:24), who pervert sex (1:26,27), and who practice the other sins listed (1:29-31) have an innate knowledge not only that these things are wrong but also that they themselves are worthy of death. They know that this is God's verdict, however much they might seek to rationalize or legalize these sins.

But this does not deter them from indulging in all these forms of ungodliness. Indeed, they unite with others to promote them, and they feel a sense of camaraderie with their partners-in-sin.

This, then, is God's answer to the question "Are the heathen lost who have never heard?" The condemnation of the heathen is that they did not live up to the light which God gave them in creation. Instead they become idolaters, and as a result they were abandoned to lives of depravity and vileness.

But suppose an individual heathen does live up to the light God gives him. Suppose he does burn his idols and seeks after the true God. What then?

There are two schools of thought among evangelical believers on this subject.

Some believe that if a pagan lives up to the light of God in creation, God will send him the gospel light. Cornelius is cited as an example. He sought after God. His prayers and alms came up as a memorial before God. Then God sent Peter to tell him how to be saved (Acts 11:14).

Others believe that if a man trusts the one true and living God as He is revealed in creation, but dies before he hears the gospel, God will save him on the basis of the work of Christ at Calvary. Even though the man himself knew nothing about the work of Christ, God reckons the value of that work to his account when he trusts God on the basis of whatever light he has received. Those who hold this view point out this is how God saved people before Calvary and how He still saves morons, imbeciles, and also children who die before they reach the age of accountability.

The first view can be supported by the case of Cornelius. The second view lacks Scriptural support for the era following the death and resurrection of Christ (our present era), and it also weakens the necessity for aggressive missionary activity.

CHAPTER 2

Paul has shown that the pagans are lost and that they need the gospel. Now he turns to a second class of people, whose exact identity is somewhat disputed by commentators. We believe that the apostle is talking here to self-righteous moralists, whether Jews or Gentiles. The first verse shows that they are self-righteous moralists by the way they condemn the behavior of others (yet commit the same sins themselves). Verses 9, 10, 12, 14, and 15 show that Paul is speaking to both Jews and Gentiles. So the question before the court is, *Are the self-righteous moralists, whether Jews or Gentiles, also lost?* And the answer, as we shall see, is, "Yes, they are lost too!"

2:1 This second class consists of those who look down their noses at the heathen, considering themselves more civilized, educated, and refined. They condemn the pagans for their gross behavior, yet are equally guilty themselves, though perhaps in a more sophisticated way.

Fallen man can see faults in others more readily than in himself. Things that are hideous and repulsive in the lives of others seem quite respectable in his own.

But the fact that he can condemn sins in others shows that he knows the difference between right and wrong. If he knows that it is wrong for someone to steal his wife, then he knows that it is wrong for him to steal someone else's wife.

Therefore, when a man commits the very sins which he condemns in others, he leaves himself without excuse.

The sins of cultured people are essentially the same as those of the heathen. Although a moralist may argue that he has not

21

committed every sin in the book, he should remember the following facts:

    a) he is capable of committing them all.

    b) by breaking one commandment, he is guilty of all (James 2:10).

    c) he has committed sins of thought which he may never have committed in actual deed, and these are forbidden by the Word. Jesus taught that the lustful look, for instance, is tantamount to adultery (Matthew 5:28).

2:2 What the smug moralist needs is a lesson on the judgment of God. The apostle proceeds to give that lesson in verses 2-16.

The first point is that *the judgment of God is according to truth*. It is not based on evidence that is incomplete, inaccurate, or circumstantial. Rather, it is based on the truth, the whole truth, and nothing but the truth.

2:3 Secondly, *the judgment of God is inescapable* on those who condemn others for the very sins they practice themselves. Their capacity to judge others does not absolve them from guilt. In fact, it increases their own condemnation.

When we say that the judgment of God is inescapable, we mean *unless those sins are repented of and forgiven*.

2:4 Next we learn that *the judgment of God is sometimes delayed*. This delay is an evidence of the goodness and forbearance and longsuffering of God. His goodness means that He is kindly disposed to sinners, though not to their sins. His forbearance describes His holding back punishment on man's wickedness and rebellion. His longsuffering is His amazing self-restraint in spite of man's ceaseless provocation.

The goodness of God, as seen in His providence, protection, and preservation, is aimed at leading men to repentance. He is "not willing that any should perish, but that all should come to repentance" (2 Peter 3:9).

Repentance means an about-face, turning one's back on sin and heading in the opposite direction. "It is a change of mind which produces a change of attitude, and results in a change of action.''[1] It signifies a man's taking sides with God against himself and his sins. It is more than an intellectual assent to the fact of one's sins; it involves the conscience too, as John Newton wrote: ''My conscience felt and owned my guilt.''

2:5 The fourth thing we learn about the judgment of God is that *it is graduated according to the accumulation of guilt*. Paul pictures hardened and unrepentant sinners stockpiling judgment for themselves, as if they were building up a fortune of gold and silver. But what a fortune that will be in the day when God's wrath is finally revealed at the judgment of the Great White Throne (Revelation 20:11-15)!

In that day *the judgment of God will be seen to be absolutely righteous*, without prejudice or injustice of any kind.

2:6 In the next five verses Paul reminds us that *the judgment of God will be according to works*. A man may boast of great personal goodness. He may rely heavily on his racial or natural origin. He may plead the fact that there were men of God in his ancestry. But he will be judged by *his own conduct*, and not by any of these other things. His works will be the determining factor.

If we were to take verses 6 through 11 by themselves, it would be easy to conclude that they teach salvation by works. They *seem* to say that those who do good works will thereby earn eternal life.

But it should be clear that the passage cannot mean that because it would then flatly contradict the consistent testimony of the rest of Scripture to the effect that salvation is by faith apart from works. Chafer points out that about 150 passages in the New Testament condition salvation solely on faith or believing.[2] No one passage, when rightly understood, can contradict such overwhelming testimony.

How then are we to understand this passage? First we must understand that good works do not begin until a person has been born again. When the people asked Jesus, ''What shall we do that we might work the works of God?'' He replied, ''This is the work of God, that ye believe on Him whom He hath sent'' (John 6:28,29). So the first good work that anyone can do is to believe on the Lord Jesus Christ, and we must constantly remember that *faith is not a meritorious work* by which a person earns salvation.

Therefore, if the unsaved are judged by their works, they will have nothing of value to present as evidence. All their supposed righteousness will be seen as filthy rags (Isaiah 64:6). Their condemning sin will be that they have not believed on Jesus as Lord (John 3:18). Beyond that, their works will determine the degree of their punishment (Luke 12:47,48).

If believers are judged according to their works, what will be the outcome? Certainly they cannot present any good works by which they might earn or deserve salvation. All their works before salvation were sinful. But the blood of Christ has wiped out the past. Now God Himself cannot find any charge against them for which to sentence them to hell. Once they are saved, they begin to practice good works—not necessarily good works in the world's eyes, but good works as God sees them. Their good works are the result of salvation, not the meritorious cause. At the Judgment Seat of Christ, their works will come into review and they will be rewarded for all faithful service.

2:7 In explaining that judgment will be according to works, Paul says that God will render eternal life to those who ''by patient continuance in well-doing seek for honor and glory and immortality.'' As already explained, this does not mean that these people are saved by patient continuance in well-doing. That would be another gospel. No one would naturally live that kind of life, and no one could live it without divine power. Anyone who really fits this description has already been saved by grace through faith. The fact that he seeks for honor and glory and incorruption shows that he has already been born again. The whole tenor of his life shows that he has been converted.

He seeks for glory, the glory of heaven; the honor that comes only from God (John 5:44); the incorruption that characterizes the resurrection body (1 Corinthians 15:53,54); the heavenly inheritance, which is imperishable, undefiled, and unfading (1 Peter 1:4).

God will award eternal life to all who manifest this evidence of a conversion experience. Eternal life is spoken of in several ways in the New Testament. It is a present possession which we receive the moment we are converted (John 5:24). It is a future possession which will be ours when we receive our glorified bodies (here and in Romans 6:22). Although it is a gift received by faith, it is sometimes associated with rewards for a life of faithfulness (Mark 10:30). All believers will have eternal life, but some will have a greater capacity for enjoying it than others. It means more than endless existence; it is a quality of life, the more abundant life which the Savior promised in John 10:10. It is the very life of Christ Himself (Colossians 1:27).

2:8 Those who are contentious or factious and who do not obey the truth, but rather obey unrighteousness, will be awarded indignation and wrath. Notice that they ''do not obey the truth''; they have never answered the gospel call. Rather, they have chosen to obey unrighteousness as their master. Their lives are characterized by strife, wrangling, and disobedience—sure proof that they were never saved.

2:9 Now the apostle repeats God's verdict concerning the two kinds of workers and works, except that this time He does it in inverse order.

The verdict will be tribulation and anguish to everyone who works evil. Here again we must stress that these evil works betray an evil heart of unbelief. The works are the outward expression of a person's attitude toward the Lord.

The expression ''to the Jew first, and also to the Greek'' (RSV) shows that *the judgment of God will be according to privilege or light received*. The Jews were first in privilege as God's chosen earthly people; therefore, they will be first in responsibility. This aspect of God's judgment will be developed further in verses 12-16.

2:10 The verdict will be glory, honor, and peace to everyone, Jew and Gentile, who works good. And let us not forget that no one can work good, as far as God is concerned, unless he has first placed his faith and trust in the Lord Jesus Christ.

The expression "to the Jew first, and also to the Gentile" cannot indicate favoritism, because the next verse points out that God's judgment is impartial. So the expression must indicate the historical order in which the gospel went out, as in 1:16. It was proclaimed first to Jews, and the first believers were Jews.

2:11 Another truth concerning the judgment of God is that *it is without respect of persons*. In human courts of law, preference is shown to the good-looking, the wealthy, and the influential; but God is strictly impartial. No considerations of race, place, or face will ever influence Him.

2:12 As mentioned above, verses 12-16 expand the point that the judgment of God will be according to the measure of light received. Two classes are in view: those who do not have the law (the Gentiles) and those who are under the law (the Jews). This includes everyone except those who are in the church of God (see 1 Corinthians 10:32, where the human race is divided into these three classes).

Those who have sinned without law shall perish without law. Notice that it does not say "shall be *judged* without law" but "shall also *perish* without law." They will be judged according to whatever revelation the Lord gave them, and, failing to live up to that revelation, they will perish.

Those who have sinned under the law will be judged by the law, and if they have not obeyed it, they too will perish.

2:13 Mere possession of the law is not enough. The law demands perfect and continuous obedience. No one is accounted righteous simply because he knows what the law says. The only conceivable way of obtaining justification under the law would be to keep it in its entirety. But since all men are sinners, it is impossible for them to do this. So this verse is really setting forth an ideal condition rather than something that is capable of human attainment.

The New Testament teaches emphatically that it is impossible for man to be justified by law-keeping (see Acts 13:39; Romans 3:20; Galatians 2:16,21; 3:11). It was never God's intention that anyone be saved by the law. Even if a person could keep it perfectly from this day forward, he still would not be justified, because God requires that which is past. So when this verse (2:13) says that doers of the law shall be justified, we must understand it as meaning that the law demands obedience, and if anyone could produce perfect obedience from the day he was born, he would be justified. But the cold, hard fact is that no one can produce this.

2:14 Verses 14 and 15 are a parenthesis, looking back to verse 12a. There we learned that Gentiles who sin without the law shall perish without the law. Now Paul explains that although the law was not given to the Gentiles, yet they have an innate knowledge of right and wrong. They know instinctively that it is wrong to lie, steal, commit adultery, and murder. The only commandment they would not know intuitively is the one concerning the Sabbath; that one is more ceremonial than moral.

So what it boils down to is that the Gentiles, who do not have the law, are a law unto themselves. They form their own code of right and wrong behavior from their moral instincts.

2:15 They show the work of the law written in their hearts. Notice that it is not the *law itself* which is written in their hearts but the *work of the law*. The work which the law was designed to do in the lives of the Israelites is seen in some measure in the lives of Gentiles. The fact that they know that it is right to respect their parents, for example, shows the work of the law written in their hearts. They also know that certain acts are basically wrong. Their conscience, serving as a monitor, confirms this instinctive knowledge. And their thoughts are constantly deciding the rightness or wrongness of their actions, excusing or accusing, allowing or forbidding.

2:16 This verse is a continuation of the thought in verse 12. It tells *when* those without law and those under the law will be judged. And in doing so it teaches one final truth about the judgment of God—namely, that *it will take into account the secrets of* *men, not just their public sin.* Sin which is secret at the present time will be open scandal at the judgment of the Great White Throne. The Judge at that solemn time will be Jesus Christ, since the Father has committed all judgment to Him (John 5:22). When Paul adds "according to my gospel," he means "so my gospel declares" (NEB). The expression "my gospel" means the gospel which Paul preached, which was also, of course, the same one which the other apostles preached.

2:17 The apostle has a third class to deal with, so now he turns to the question: *Are the Jews, to whom the law was given, also lost?* And of course the answer is, "Yes, they are lost too!"

There is no doubt that many Jews felt they were immune from God's judgment. God would never send a Jew to hell, they thought. The Gentiles, on the other hand, were fuel for the flames of hell. Paul must now destroy this pretension by showing that under certain circumstances Gentiles may be closer to God than Jews.

First he reviews those things which a Jew prized as giving him an inside track with God.

He bore the name of a Jew and thus was a member of God's chosen earthly people.

He rested upon the law, which was never designed to give rest but rather to awaken the conscience to a sense of sinfulness.

He gloried in God, the only true God, who had entered into a unique covenant relationship with the nation of Israel.

2:18 He knew God's will, because a general outline of that will is given in the Scriptures.

He approved the things that are excellent, because the law taught him how to assess moral values.

2:19 He prided himself on being a guide of those who were morally and spiritually blind, a light to those who were in the darkness of ignorance.

2:20 He felt qualified to correct the foolish or untaught and to teach babes, because the law gave him an outline of knowledge and of the truth.

2:21 But these things in which the Jew boasted had never changed his life. It was simply pride of race, religion, and knowledge without any corresponding moral transformation. He taught others but did not take the lessons to heart himself. He preached against stealing but did not practice what he preached.

2:22 When he forbade adultery, it was a case of "Do as I say, not as I do." While he loathed and abhorred idols, he didn't hesitate to rob temples, perhaps by actually looting heathen shrines.

2:23 He gloried in the possession of the law, but he dishonored the God who gave it by breaking its sacred precepts.

2:24 This combination of high talk and low walk caused the Gentiles to blaspheme the name of God. They judged the Lord, as men always do, by those who professed to be His followers. It was true in Isaiah's day (Isaiah 52:5) and it is still true today. Each of us should ask,

> If of Jesus Christ their only view
> May be what they see of Him in you,
> (Insert your name), what do they see?

2:25 In addition to the law, the Jew prided himself on the rite of circumcision. This was a minor surgical operation performed on the foreskin of the Jewish male. It was instituted by God as a sign of His covenant with Abraham (Genesis 17:9-14). It expressed the separation of a people to God from the world. After a while the Jews so prided themselves on having had the operation that they contemptuously called the Gentiles "the uncircumcision."

Here Paul links circumcision with the Law of Moses and points out that it was only valid as a sign when it was combined with a life of obedience. God is not a mere ritualist; He is not satisfied with external ceremonies unless they are accompanied by inward holiness. So a circumcised Jew who transgresses the law might just as well be uncircumcised.

When the apostle speaks about keepers or doers of the law in this passage, we must not take the words in an absolute sense.

2:26 Thus, if a Gentile adheres to the morality prescribed by the law, even if he isn't under the law, his uncircumcision is more acceptable than the circumcision of a Jewish transgressor. In such a case the Gentile's heart is circumcised, and that is what counts.

2:27 In such a case the superior behavior of the Gentile condemns the Jew who has the law and circumcision but who does not keep the law or live the circumcised life, the life of separation and sanctification.

2:28 In God's reckoning, a true Jew is not simply a man who has Abraham's blood flowing in his veins or who has the mark of circumcision in his body. A person may have both these things and be the scum of the earth morally. The Lord is not swayed by external considerations of race or religion; He looks for inward sincerity and purity.

2:29 The real Jew is the one who is not only a descendant of Abraham but who also manifests a godly life. This passage does not teach that all believers are Jews, or that the church is the Israel of God. Paul is talking about those who are born of Jewish parentage and is insisting that the mere fact of birth and the ordinance of circumcision are not enough. There must also be inward reality.

True circumcision is a matter of the heart—not just a literal cutting of the body but the spiritual reality of surgery on the old, unregenerate nature.

Those who thus combine the outward sign and the inward grace receive God's praise, if not man's. There is a play on words in this last verse that is not apparent in the English. The word "Jew" comes from "Judah," meaning praise. A real Jew is one whose character is such as to receive praise from God.

CHAPTER 3

3:1 Paul continues the subject of the guilt of the Jews in the first eight verses of this chapter. Here a Jewish objector appears and begins to cross-examine the apostle. The questioning proceeds as follows.

OBJECTOR: If all you have said in 2:17-29 is true, then what is the superiority of being a Jew and what benefit is there from circumcision?

3:2 PAUL: The Jews have had many special privileges. The most important is that they were entrusted with the oracles of God. The Old Testament Scriptures were given to Jews to write and to preserve, but how have the people of Israel responded to this tremendous privilege? On the whole, they have demonstrated an appalling lack of faith.

3:3 OBJECTOR: Well, granted that not all Jews have believed, but does this mean that God will go back on His promises? After all, He did choose Israel as His people and He made definite covenants with them. Can the unbelief of some cause God to break His Word?

3:4 PAUL: Don't even suggest such a thing! Whenever there is a question whether God or man is right, always proceed on the basis that God is right and every man is a liar. This is what David said, in effect, in Psalm 51:4: ''The complete truthfulness of all You say must be defended, and You must be vindicated every time You are called into question by sinful man.'' Our sins only serve to confirm the truthfulness of God's words.

3:5 OBJECTOR: If that's the case, why does God condemn us?

31

If our unrighteousness causes the righteousness of God to shine more gloriously, how can God visit us with wrath?

(Paul notes here that in quoting these words, he is using a typically human argument.)

3:6 PAUL: Such an argument is unworthy of serious consideration. If there were any possibility of God's being unrighteous, then how could He be fit to judge the world? Yet we all admit that He *will* judge the world.

3:7 OBJECTOR: But if my sin brings glory to God, if my lie vindicates His truth, if He causes man's wrath to praise Him, then how can He consistently find fault with me as a sinner?

3:8 Why wouldn't it be logical to say—
PAUL: Let me interrupt to say that some people actually accuse us Christians of using this argument, but it is a slander.
OBJECTOR: Why wouldn't it be logical to say, "Let us do evil, that good may come"?
PAUL: All I can say is that the condemnation of people who talk like that is well-deserved.

(Actually this last argument, stupid as it seems, is constantly leveled against the gospel of the grace of God. People say, "If you could be saved just by faith in Christ, then you could go out and live in sin. Since God's grace superabounds over man's sin, then the more you sin, the more His grace abounds." The apostle answers this objection in chapter 6.)

3:9 OBJECTOR: Are you saying, then, that we Jews are no better than those sinful Gentiles? Or the question may be, according to some versions, "Are we Jews worse than the Gentiles?" (See the margin of RSV, NIV, NEB.) The answer in either case is that the Jews are no better and no worse. All are sinners.

That leads up to and parallels the next question in Paul's presentation. He has shown that the heathen are lost; the self-righteous moralists, whether Jews or Gentiles, are lost; the Jews are lost. Now he turns to the question: *Are all men lost?*

The answer is, "Yes, we have already charged that all men

are slaves to sin,'' and this means that Jews are no different from Gentiles in this respect.

3:10 If further proof is needed, that proof is found in the Old Testament Scriptures. First we see that sin has affected everyone born of human parents (3:10-12) and then we see that sin has affected every part of a man (3:13-18). We might paraphrase it as follows: ''There is not one righteous person'' (Psalm 14:1).

3:11 ''There is no one who has a right understanding of God. There is no one who seeks after God'' (Psalm 14:2). If left to himself, fallen man would never seek after God. It is only through the work of the Holy Spirit that anyone ever does.

3:12 ''All have gone astray from God. All mankind has become corrupt. There is not one who lives a good life, no, not one'' (Psalm 14:3).

3:13 ''Men's throats are like an opened tomb. Their speech has been consistently deceitful'' (Psalm 5:9). ''Their conversation flows from poisonous lips'' (Psalm 140:3).

3:14 ''Their mouths are full of cursing and hatred'' (Psalm 10:7).

3:15 ''Their feet are swift to carry them on missions of murder'' (Isaiah 59:7).

3:16 ''They leave a trail of ruin and misery'' (Isaiah 59:7).

3:17 ''They have never known how to make peace'' (Isaiah 59:8).

3:18 ''They have no respect for God'' (Psalm 36:1).

This, then, is God's x-ray of the human race. It reveals universal unrighteousness (3:10); ignorance and independence toward God (3:11); waywardness, unprofitableness, and lack of any goodness (3:12). Man's throat is full of rottenness, his tongue is deceitful, his lips are venomous (3:13), his mouth is full of swearing (3:14), his feet are bent on murder (3:15), he leaves behind trouble and destruction (3:16), he doesn't know how to make peace (3:17), and he has no regard for God (3:18). Here we see the total depravity of man, by which we mean that sin has affected all of mankind and that it has affected every part of his being. We do not mean that every man has committed every sin, but that he has a nature which is capable of committing them all.

If Paul had wanted to give a more complete catalog of sins, he could have mentioned the sins of sex: adultery, homosexuality, lesbianism, perversion, bestiality, prostitution, rape, lewdness, pornography, and smut. He could have mentioned the sins associated with war: destruction of innocents, atrocities, gas chambers, ovens, concentration camps, torture devices, sadism. He could have mentioned sins of the home: unfaithfulness, divorce, wife-beating, mental cruelty, child abuse. Add to these the crimes of murder, mutilation, theft, burglary, embezzlement, vandalism, graft, corruption. Also the sins of speech: profanity, suggestive jokes, sensual language, cursing, blasphemy, lies, backbiting, gossip, character assassination, grumbling, and complaining. Other personal sins are: drunkenness, drug addiction, pride, envy, covetousness, ingratitude, filthy thought-life, hatred, and bitterness. The list is seemingly endless—pollution, littering, racism, exploitation, deceit, betrayal, broken promises, and on and on. What further proof of human depravity is needed?

3:19 When God gave the law to Israel, He was using Israel as a sample of the human race. He found that Israel was a failure, and He correctly applied this finding to all of humanity. It is the same as when a health inspector takes a test-tube of water from a well, tests the sample, finds it polluted, and then pronounces the entire well polluted.

So Paul explains that when the law speaks, it speaks to those who are under the law—the people of Israel—in order that *every mouth, Jew and Gentile,* may be stopped, and *all the world* be brought in guilty before God.

3:20 No one can be justified by keeping the law. The law was not given to justify people but to produce the knowledge of sin—not the knowledge of *salvation,* but the knowledge of *sin.*

We could never know what a crooked line is unless we also knew a straight line. The law is like a straight line. When men test themselves by it, they see how crooked they are.

We can use a mirror to see that our face is dirty, but the mirror is not designed to wash the dirty face.

A thermometer will tell whether a person has a fever, but swallowing the thermometer will not cure the fever.

The law is good when it is used to produce conviction of sin, but it is worthless as a savior from sin.

3:21 We now come to the heart of the Letter to the Romans, when Paul answers the question: *According to the gospel, how can ungodly sinners be justified by a holy God?*

He begins by saying that the righteousness of God has been revealed apart from the law. This means that a plan or program has been revealed by which God can righteously save unrighteous sinners, and that it is not by requiring men to keep the law. Because God is holy, He cannot condone sin or overlook it or wink at it. He must punish it. And the punishment for sin is death. Yet God loves the sinner and wants to save him; there is the dilemma. God's righteousness demands the sinner's death, but His love desires the sinner's eternal happiness. The gospel reveals how God can save sinners without compromising His righteousness.

This righteous plan is witnessed by the law and the prophets. It was foretold in the types and shadows of the sacrificial system that required the shedding of blood for atonement. And it was foretold by direct prophecies (see, for example, Isaiah 51:5,6,8; 56:1; Daniel 9:16,24).

3:22 The previous verse told us that this righteous salvation is *not* obtained on the basis of law-keeping. Now the apostle tells us how it *is* obtained—through faith in Jesus Christ. Faith here means utter reliance on the living Lord Jesus Christ as one's only Savior from sin and one's only hope for heaven. It is based on the revelation of the Person and work of Christ as found in the Bible.

Faith is not a leap in the dark. It demands the surest evidence, and finds it in the infallible Word of God.

Faith is not illogical or unreasonable. What is more reasonable than that the creature should trust his Creator?

Faith is not a meritorious work by which a man earns or deserves salvation. A man cannot boast because he has believed the Lord; he would be a fool *not* to believe Him. Faith is not an attempt to earn salvation, but is the simple acceptance of the salvation which God offers as a free gift.

Paul goes on to tell us that this salvation is "unto all and upon all them that believe." It is "unto all" in the sense that it is available to all, offered to all, and sufficient for all. But it is only *upon* those who believe; that is, it is effective only in the lives of those who accept the Lord Jesus by a definite act of faith. The pardon is for all, but it becomes valid in an individual's life only when he accepts it. (It should be noted that the words "upon all" are omitted in some manuscripts.)

When Paul says that salvation is available to all, he includes Gentiles as well as Jews, because now there is no difference. The Jew has no special privilege and the Gentile is at no disadvantage.

3:23 The availability of the gospel is as universal as the need. And the need is universal because all have sinned and come short of the glory of God. All have sinned in Adam; when he sinned, he acted as the representative for all his descendants. But men are not only sinners by nature; they are also sinners by *practice*. They come short, in themselves, of the glory of God.

That is what sin is. It is any thought, word, or deed that falls short of God's standard of holiness and perfection. It is a missing of the mark, a coming short of the target. An Indian whose arrow fell short of its target was heard to say, "Oh, I sinned." In his language the same word was used to express sinning and falling short of the target.

Sin is lawlessness (1 John 3:4 NASB), the rebellion of the creature's will against the will of God.

Sin is not only doing what is wrong but the failure to do what one knows to be right (James 4:17).

Whatever is not of faith is sin (Romans 14:23). This means that it is wrong for a man to do anything about which he has a reasonable doubt. If he does not have a clear conscience about it, and yet goes ahead and does it, he is sinning.

All unrighteousness is sin (1 John 5:17). And the thought of foolishness is sin (Proverbs 24:9). Sin begins in the mind. When encouraged and entertained, it breaks forth into an act, and the act leads on to death.

Sin is often attractive when first contemplated, but hideous in retrospect.

Sometimes Paul distinguishes between sins and sin. Sins refer to wrong things that we have done. Sin refers to our evil nature—that is, to what we are. What we *are* is a lot worse than anything we have ever done. But Christ died for our evil nature as well as for our evil deeds. God forgives our sins, but the Bible never speaks of His forgiving our sin. Instead, He *condemns* or *judges* sin in the flesh (Romans 8:3).

There is also a difference between sin and transgression. Transgression is a violation of a known law. Stealing is basically sinful; it is wrong in itself. But stealing is also a transgression when there is a law that forbids it. "Where no law is, there is no transgression" (Romans 4:15).

Paul has shown that all men have sinned and continually come short of God's glory. Now he goes on to present the remedy.

3:24 "Being justified freely by his grace." The gospel tells how God justifies sinners as a free gift and by an act of unmerited favor. But what do we mean when we speak of the act of justifying?

The word *justify* means to reckon or declare to be righteous. For example, God pronounces a sinner to be righteous when that sinner believes on the Lord Jesus Christ. This is the way the word is most often used in the New Testament.

However, a man can justify God (see Luke 7:29) by believing and obeying God's Word. In other words, he declares God to be righteous in all that God says and does.

And, of course, a man can justify himself; that is, he can protest his own righteousness (see Luke 10:29). But this is nothing but a form of self-deception.

To justify does not mean to actually *make* a person righteous. We cannot *make* God righteous; He already *is* righteous. But we can *declare* Him to be righteous. God does not *make* the believer sinless or righteous in himself. Rather, God puts righteousness to his account. As A. T. Pierson put it, "God, in justifying sinners, actually calls them righteous when they are not, does not impute sin where sin actually exists, and does impute righteousness where it does not exist."[1]

A popular definition of justification is *just as if I'd never sinned*. But this does not go far enough. When God justifies the believing sinner, He not only acquits him from guilt but clothes him in His own righteousness and thus makes him absolutely fit for heaven. "Justification goes beyond acquittal to approval; beyond pardon to promotion."[2] Acquittal means only that a person is set free from a charge. Justification means that positive righteousness is imputed.

The reason God can declare ungodly sinners to be righteous is because the Lord Jesus Christ has fully paid the debt of their sins by His death and resurrection. When sinners accept Christ by faith, they are justified.

When James teaches that justification is by works (James 2:24), he does not mean that we are saved by good works, or by faith plus good works, but rather by the kind of faith that results in good works.

It is important to realize that justification is a reckoning that takes place in the mind of God. It is not something a believer feels; he knows it has taken place because the Bible says so. C. I. Scofield expressed it this way: "Justification is that act of God whereby He declares righteous all who believe in Jesus. It is something which takes place in the mind of God, not in the nervous system or emotional nature of the believer."

Here in Romans 3:24 the apostle teaches that we are justified freely. It is not something we can earn or purchase, but rather something that is offered as a gift.

Next we learn that we are justified by God's grace. This simply means that it is wholly apart from any merit in ourselves.

As far as we are concerned, it is undeserved, unsought, and unbought.

In order to avoid confusion later on, we should pause here to explain that there are six different aspects of justification in the New Testament. We are said to be justified by grace, by faith, by blood, by power, by God, and by works; yet there is no contradiction or conflict.

We are justified by grace—that means we do not deserve it.

We are justified by faith (Romans 5:1)—that means that we have to receive it by believing on the Lord Jesus Christ.

We are justified by blood (Romans 5:9)—that refers to the price the Savior paid in order that we might be justified.

We are justified by power (Romans 4:25)—the same power that raised the Lord Jesus from the dead.

We are justified by God (Romans 8:33)—He is the One who reckons us righteous.

We are justified by works (James 2:24)—not meaning that good works earn justification, but that they are the evidence that we have been justified.

Returning to 3:24, we read that we are justified ''through the redemption that is in Christ Jesus.'' Redemption means buying back by the paying of a ransom price. The Lord Jesus bought us back from the slave market of sin. His precious blood was the ransom price which was paid to satisfy the claims of a holy and righteous God. If someone asks, ''To whom was the ransom paid?'' he misses the point. The Scriptures nowhere suggest that a specific payment was made either to God or to Satan. The ransom was not paid to anyone but was an abstract settlement that provided a righteous basis by which God could save the ungodly.

3:25 God has set forth Christ Jesus to be a propitiation. A propitiation is a means by which justice is satisfied, God's wrath is averted, and mercy can be shown on the basis of an acceptable sacrifice.

Three times in the New Testament Christ is spoken of as a propitiation. Here in Romans 3:25 we learn that those who put their faith in Christ find mercy by virtue of His shed blood. In

1 John 2:2 Christ is described as the propitiation for our sins, and for those of the whole world. His work is sufficient for the whole world but is only effective for those who put their trust in Him. Finally, in 1 John 4:10, God's love was manifested in sending His Son to be the propitiation for our sins.

The prayer of the publican in Luke 18:13 was literally "God be propitious to me, the sinner." He was asking God to show mercy to him by not requiring him to pay the penalty of his aggravated guilt.

The word "propitiation" also occurs in Hebrews 2:17 NASB: "Therefore He had to be made like His brethren in all things, that He might become a merciful and faithful high priest in things pertaining to God, to make propitiation for the sins of the people." Here the expression "to make propitiation" means to put away by paying the penalty.

The Old Testament equivalent of the word *propitiation* is *mercy-seat*. You will remember that the mercy-seat was the lid of the ark. On the Day of Atonement the high priest sprinkled the mercy-seat with the blood of a sacrificial victim. By this means the errors of the high priest and of the people were atoned for or covered.

When Christ made propitiation for our sins, He went much further. He not only *covered them* but *put them away completely*.

Now Paul tells us in 3:25 that God has set Christ forth to be a propitiation through faith, in His blood. Notice the comma we have put after *faith* in the preceding sentence. We are not told to put our faith in His blood; *Christ Himself* is the object of our faith. It is only a resurrected and living Christ Jesus who can save. He is the propitiation. Faith in Him is the condition by which we avail ourselves of the propitiation. His blood is the price that was paid.

The finished work of Christ declares God's righteousness for the remission of sins that are past. This refers to sins committed before the death of Christ. From Adam to Christ, God saved those who put their faith in Him on the basis of whatever revelation He gave them. Abraham, for example, believed God, and it was reckoned to him for righteousness (Genesis 15:6). But how could

God do this righteously? A sinless Substitute had not been slain. The blood of a perfect Sacrifice had not been shed. In a word, Christ had not died. The debt had not been paid. God's righteous claims had not been met. How then could God save believing sinners in the Old Testament period?

The answer is that although Christ had not yet died, God knew that He *would* die, and He saved men on the basis of the still-future work of Christ. Even if Old Testament saints didn't know about Calvary, God knew about it, and He put all the value of Christ's work to their account when they believed God. In a very real sense, Old Testament believers were saved on credit. They were saved on the basis of a price still to be paid. They looked forward to Calvary; we look back to it.

That is what Paul means when he says that the propitiation of Christ declares God's righteousness because of the passing by of the sins done in previous times. He is not speaking, as some wrongly think, of sins which an individual person has committed before his conversion. This might suggest that the work of Christ took care of sins before the new birth, but that a man is on his own after that. No, he is dealing with the seeming leniency of God in apparently overlooking the sins of those who were saved before the Cross. It might seem that God excused those sins or pretended not to see them. Not so, says Paul. The Lord knew that Christ would make full expiation, and so He saved men on that basis.

Actually this was not a problem to God (as it is to us). He does not live in the realm of time. Time is a matter of the relationship of the earth to the sun. He lives above all such relationships. To Him Calvary is an ever-present reality. And Christ is the Lamb slain from the foundation of the world (Revelation 13:8).

So the Old Testament period was a time of the forbearance of God. For at least 4000 years He held back His judgment on sin. Then in the fullness of time He sent His Son to be the Sin-bearer. When the Lord Jesus took our sins upon Himself, God unleashed the full fury of His righteous, holy wrath on the Son of His love.

3:26 Now the death of Christ declares God's righteousness. God is just because He has required the full payment of the penalty of sin. And He can justify the ungodly without condoning their sin or compromising His own righteousness because a perfect Substitute has died and risen again. Albert Midlane has stated the truth in poetry:

> The perfect righteousness of God
> Is witnessed in the Savior's blood;
> 'Tis in the cross of Christ we trace
> His righteousness, yet wondrous grace.
>
> God could not pass the sinner by,
> His sin demands that he must die;
> But in the cross of Christ we see
> How God can save, yet righteous be.
>
> The sin is on the Savior laid,
> 'Tis in His blood sin's debt is paid;
> Stern justice can demand no more,
> And mercy can dispense her store.
>
> The sinner who believes is free,
> Can say, "The Savior died for me";
> Can point to the atoning blood,
> And say, "That made my peace with God."

3:27 Where, then, is boasting in this wonderful plan of salvation? It is shut out, excluded, banned. By what principle is boasting excluded? By the principle of works? No. If salvation were by works, that would allow room for all kinds of self-congratulation. But when salvation is on the principle of faith, there is no room for boasting. The justified person says, "I did all the sinning; Jesus did all the saving." True faith disavows any possibility of self-help, self-improvement, or self-salvation, looking only to Christ as Savior. Its language is:

> In my hand no price I bring,
> Simply to Thy cross I cling;

> Naked, come to Thee for dress,
> Helpless, look to Thee for grace.
> Foul, I to the fountain fly;
> Wash me, Savior, or I die.
> —Augustus M. Toplady

3:28 As the reason why boasting is excluded, Paul reiterates that man is justified by faith apart from the works of the law.

3:29 How does the gospel present God? Is He the exclusive God of the Jews? No, He is the God of the Gentiles also. The Lord Jesus Christ did not die for one race of mankind but for the whole world of sinners. And the offer of full and free salvation goes out to whosoever will, Jew or Gentile.

3:30 There aren't two Gods—one for the Jews and one for the Gentiles. There is only one God and only one way of salvation for all mankind. He justifies the circumcision by faith and the uncircumcision through faith. Whatever the reason for the use of different prepositions here (*by* and *through*), there is no difference in the instrumental cause of justification; it is faith in both cases.

3:31 An important question remains. When we say that salvation is by faith and not by law-keeping, do we imply that the law is worthless and should be disregarded? Does the gospel wave the law aside as if it had no place? On the contrary, the gospel establishes the law, and this is how.

The law demands perfect obedience. The penalty for breaking the law must be paid. That penalty is DEATH. If a lawbreaker pays the penalty, he will be lost eternally. The gospel tells how Christ died to pay the penalty of the broken law. He did not treat it as a thing to be ignored. He paid the debt in full. Now anyone who has broken the law can avail himself of the fact that Christ paid the penalty on his behalf. Thus the gospel of salvation by faith upholds the law by insisting that its utmost demands must be and have been fully met.

CHAPTER 4

The fifth main question that Paul takes up is: *Does the gospel agree with the teachings of the Old Testament Scriptures?*

The answer to this question would be of special importance to the Jewish people. Therefore the apostle now shows that there is complete harmony between the gospel in the New Testament and in the Old Testament. Justification has always been by faith.

4:1 Paul proves his point by referring to two of the greatest figures in Israel's history: Abraham and David. God made great covenants with both these men. One lived centuries before the law was given, and the other lived many years afterward. One was justified before he was circumcised, and the other after.

Let us first consider Abraham, of whom all Jews could say "our forefather according to the flesh." What was his experience? What did he find concerning the way in which a person is justified?

4:2 If Abraham was justified by works, then he would have reason for boasting. He could pat himself on the back for earning a righteous standing before God. But this is utterly impossible. No one will ever be able to boast before God (Ephesians 2:9). There is nothing in the Scriptures to indicate that Abraham had any grounds for boasting that he was justified by his works.

But someone may argue, "Doesn't it say in James 2:21 that Abraham was justified by works?" Yes it does, but there the meaning is quite different. Abraham was justified by faith in Genesis 15:6 when he believed God's promise concerning a numberless posterity. It was 30 or more years later that he was justified (vindicated) by works when he started to offer Isaac as a burnt offering to God (Genesis 22). This act of obedience proved

44

the reality of his faith. It was an outward demonstration that he had been truly justified by faith.

4:3 What do the Scriptures say concerning his justification? They say, ''He believed in the Lord; and He counted it to him for righteousness'' (Genesis 15:6). God revealed Himself to Abraham and promised that he would have a numberless posterity. The patriarch believed in the Lord, and God put righteousness to his account. In other words, Abraham was justified by faith. It was just as simple as that. Works had nothing to do with it. They aren't even mentioned.

4:4 All of this brings us to one of the sublimest statements in the Bible concerning the contrast between works and faith in reference to the plan of salvation.

Think of it this way: when a man works for a living and gets his paycheck at the end of the week, he is entitled to his wages. He has earned them. He does not bow and scrape before his employer, thanking him for such a display of kindness and protesting that he doesn't deserve the money. Not at all! He puts the money in his pocket and goes home with the feeling that he has only been reimbursed for his time and labor.

But that's not the way it is in the matter of justification.

4:5 Shocking as it may seem, the justified man is the one who, first of all, doesn't work. He renounces any possibility of earning his salvation. He disavows any personal merit or goodness. He acknowledges that all his best labors could never fulfill God's righteous demands.

Instead, he believes on Him who justifies the ungodly. He puts his faith and trust in the Lord. He takes God at His Word. As we have seen, this is not a meritorious action. The merit is not in his faith, but in *the Object of his faith*.

Notice that he believes on Him who justifies *the ungodly*. He doesn't come with the plea that he has tried his best, that he has lived by the Golden Rule, that he has not been as bad as others. No, he comes as an ungodly, guilty sinner and throws himself on the mercy of God.

And what is the result? His faith is reckoned unto him for righteousness. Because he has come believing instead of working, God puts righteousness to his account. Through the merits of the risen Savior, God clothes him with righteousness and thus makes him fit for heaven. Henceforth God sees him in Christ and accepts him on that basis.

To summarize, then, justification is for the ungodly—not for good people. It is a matter of grace—not of debt. And it is received by faith—not by works.

4:6 Next Paul turns to David to prove his thesis. The words "even as" at the beginning of this verse indicate that David's experience was the same as Abraham's. The sweet singer of Israel said that the happy man is the sinner whom God reckons righteous apart from works. Although David never said this in so many words, the apostle derives it from Psalm 32:1,2, which he quotes in the next two verses.

4:7 Blessed is he whose transgression is forgiven, whose sin is covered.

4:8 Blessed is the man unto whom the Lord imputeth not iniquity.

What did Paul see in these verses? First of all, he noticed that David said nothing about works; forgiveness is a matter of God's grace, not of man's efforts. Second, he saw that if God doesn't impute sin to a person, then that person must have a righteous standing before Him. Finally, he saw that God justifies *the ungodly;* David has been guilty of adultery and murder, yet in these verses he is tasting the sweetness of full and free pardon.

4:9 But the idea may still lurk in some Jewish minds that the chosen people had a corner on God's justification, that only those who were circumcised could be justified. The apostle turns again to the experience of Abraham to show that this is not so. He poses the question, "Is righteousness imputed to believing Jews only, or to believing Gentiles as well?" The fact that Abraham was used as an example might seem to suggest that it was only to Jews.

4:10 Here Paul seizes on a historical fact that most of us would never have noticed. He shows that Abraham was justified (Genesis 15:6) before he was ever circumcised (Genesis 17:24). If the father of the nation of Israel could be justified while he was still uncircumcised, then the question remains, ''Why can't any other uncircumcised people be justified?'' In a very real sense, Abraham was justified while still on Gentile ground, and this leaves the door wide open for other Gentiles to be justified, entirely apart from circumcision.

4:11 Circumcision, then, was not the instrumental cause of Abraham's justification. It was merely an outward sign in his flesh that he had been justified by faith. Basically, circumcision was the external token of the covenant between God and the people of Israel; but here its meaning is expanded to indicate the righteousness which God imputed to Abraham through faith.

In addition to being a sign, circumcision was a seal—''a seal of the righteousness of the faith which he had yet being uncircumcised.'' The sign points to the existence of that which it signifies. The seal authenticates, confirms, certifies, or guarantees the genuineness of that which is signified. Circumcision confirmed to Abraham that he was regarded and treated by God as righteous through faith.

Circumcision was a seal of the righteousness of Abraham's faith. This may mean that his faith was righteous or it may mean that he obtained righteousness through faith. The latter is almost certainly the correct meaning; circumcision was a seal of the righteousness which belonged to his faith or which he obtained on the basis of faith.

Because Abraham was justified before he was circumcised, he can be the father of other uncircumcised people—that is, of believing Gentiles. They can be justified the same way he was—by faith.

When it says that Abraham is the father of believing Gentiles, there is no thought of physical descent, of course. It simply means that these believers are his children because they imitate his faith. They are not his children by birth but by following him as their pattern, model, and example. Neither does the passage teach that believing Gentiles become the Israel of God. The Israel of God is composed of those Jews who accept Jesus, the Messiah, as their Lord and Savior.

4:12 Abraham received the sign of circumcision for another reason also—namely, that he might be the father of those Jews who are not only circumcised but who follow his footsteps in a path of faith, the kind of faith which he had before he was ever circumcised.

There is a difference between being Abraham's seed and Abraham's children. Jesus said to the Pharisees, "I know that ye are Abraham's seed [descendants]" (John 8:37). But then He went on to say, "If ye were Abraham's children, ye would do the works of Abraham" (John 8:39). So here Paul insists that physical circumcision is not what counts. There must be faith in the living God. Those of the circumcision who believe in the Lord Jesus Christ are the true Israel of God.

To summarize, then, there was a time in Abraham's life when he had faith and was uncircumcised, and another time when he had faith and was circumcised. Paul's eagle eye sees in this the fact that both believing Gentiles and believing Jews can claim Abraham as their father and can identify with him as his children.

4:13 "The argument continues relentlessly on as Paul chases every possible objector down every possible alleyway of logic and Scripture."[1] The apostle now must deal with the objection that blessing came through the law and that therefore the Gentiles who did not have the law were cursed (see John 7:49).

When God promised Abraham and his seed that he would be heir of the world, He did not make the promise conditional on adherence to some legal code. (The law itself wasn't given until 430 years later—Galatians 3:17.) It was an unconditional promise of grace, to be received by faith—the same kind of faith by which we obtain God's righteousness today.

The expression "heir of the world" means that he would be the father of believing Gentiles as well as of Jews (4:11,12), that he would be the father of many nations (4:17,18) and not just of the Jewish nation. In its fullest sense the promise will be fulfilled when the Lord Jesus, Abraham's seed, takes the scepter of universal empire and reigns as King of kings and Lord of lords.

4:14 If those who seek God's blessing, and particularly the blessing of justification, are able to inherit it on the basis of law-keeping, then faith is set aside and the promise is worthless. Faith is set aside because it is a principle that is completely opposite to law: faith is a matter of *believing,* while law is a matter of *doing.* The promise would then be worthless because it would be based on conditions that no one would be able to meet.

4:15 The law works God's wrath, not His blessing. It condemns those who fail to keep its commandments perfectly and continuously. And since none can do that, all who are under the law are condemned to death. It is impossible to be under the law without being under the curse.

But where there is no law, there is no transgression. Transgression means the violation of a known law. Paul does not say that where there is no law, there is no sin. An act can be inherently wrong even if there is no law against it. But it becomes transgression when there is a law that forbids it. It is wrong to speed down a street at 90 miles per hour when children are getting out of school. But it becomes transgression when a sign goes up saying ''Speed Limit 20 MPH.''

The Jews thought they inherited blessing through having the law, but all they inherited was transgression. God gave the law so that sin might be seen as transgression, or to put it another way, so that sin might be seen in all its sinfulness. He never intended it to be the way of salvation for sinful transgressors.

4:16 Because law produces God's wrath and not His justification, God determined that He would save men by grace through faith. He would give eternal life as a free, undeserved gift to ungodly sinners who receive it by a simple act of faith.

In this way the promise of life is sure to all the seed. We should underline two words here—*sure* and *all.* First, God wants the promise to be *sure.* If justification depended on man's law—works, he could never be sure because he could not know if he had done enough good works or the right kind. No one who seeks to earn salvation enjoys full assurance. But when salvation is presented as a gift to be received by believing, then a man can be sure that he is saved on the authority of the Word of God.

Second, God wants the promise to be sure to *all* the seed—not just to the Jews, to whom the law was given, but also to Gentiles who put their trust in the Lord in the same way that Abraham did. Abraham is the father of us all—that is, of all believing Jews and Gentiles.

4:17 To confirm Abraham's fatherhood over all true believers, Paul injects Genesis 17:5 as a parenthesis: "I have made thee a father of many nations." God's choice of Israel as His chosen, earthly people did not mean that His grace and mercy would be confined to them. The apostle ingeniously quotes verse after verse from the Old Testament to show that it was always God's intention to honor faith wherever He found it.

The phrase "before him whom he believed" continues the thought from 4:16: ". . . Abraham, who is the father of us all." The connection is this: Abraham is the father of us all in the sight of Him (God) whom he (Abraham) believed, even God who gives life to the dead and speaks of things that do not yet exist as already existing. To understand this description of God, we have only to look at the verses that follow. God gives life to the dead—that is, to Abraham and Sarah, for although they were not dead physically, they were childless and beyond the age when they could have children (see 4:19). God calls things not yet existing as already existing—that is, a numberless posterity involving many nations (see 4:18).

4:18 In the preceding verses the apostle has emphasized that the promise came to Abraham by faith and not by law that it might be by grace and that it might be sure to all the seed. That leads quite naturally to a consideration of Abraham's faith in the God of resurrection.

God promised Abraham posterity as numberless as the stars and the sand. Humanly speaking, the chances were all but hopeless. But against human hope, Abraham believed, in hope that he would be the father of many nations, just as God had promised in Genesis 15:5: "So shall thy seed be."

4:19 When the promise of a great posterity was first made to Abraham, he was 75 years old (Genesis 12:2-4). At that time he was still physically able to become a father, because after that he begat Ishmael (Genesis 16:1-11). But in this verse Paul is speaking of the time when Abraham was about 100 years old and the promise was renewed (Genesis 17:15-21). By now the possibility of creating new life apart from the miraculous power of God had vanished. However, God had promised him a son, and Abraham believed God's promise.

Without being weakened in faith, he considered his own body, and his conclusion was "as good as dead" (NASB). He considered Sarah's womb, and his conclusion was "dead also." He made a realistic appraisal of the situation and concluded that, humanly speaking, it was utterly hopeless.

We should pause here to mention that some versions, such as the King James Version, say, ". . . he considered *not* his own body now dead . . . *neither* the deadness of Sara's womb." But the negatives ("not" and "neither") are not found in the best manuscripts. Abraham did face up to the hopelessness of the situation, but in spite of it he believed the promises of God.

4:20 The apparent impossibility that the promise would ever be fulfilled didn't stagger him. God had said it; Abraham believed it; that settled it. As far as the patriarch was concerned there was only one impossibility, and that was for God to lie. Abraham's faith was strong and vibrant. He gave glory to God, honoring Him as the One who could be depended on to fulfill His promise in defiance of all the laws of chance or probability.

4:21 Abraham did not know how God would fulfill His Word, but that was incidental. He knew God and had every confidence that God was fully able to do what He had promised.

In one way it was wonderful faith, but in another way it was the most reasonable thing to do, because God's Word is the surest thing in the universe, and for Abraham there was no risk in believing it!

4:22 God was pleased to find a man who took Him at His Word; He always is. And so he credited righteousness to Abraham's account. Where once there had been a balance of sin and guilt, now there was nothing but a righteous standing before God. Abraham had been delivered from condemnation and was justified by a holy God through faith.

4:23 The historical narrative of his justification by faith was not written for his sake alone. There was a sense, of course, in which it was written for his sake—a permanent record of his acquittal and his now-perfect standing before God.

4:24 But it was written for our benefit too. Our faith is likewise reckoned for righteousness when we believe on God, who raised Jesus our Lord from the dead. The only difference is this: Abraham believed that God *would* give life to the dead (that is, to his weak body and Sarah's barren womb). We believe that God *has* given life to the dead by raising the Lord Jesus Christ. ''Abraham was called to believe in a promise, whereas we are privileged to believe in an accomplished fact. He was called to look forward to something which was to be done; we look back on something that is done, even an accomplished redemption, attested by the fact of a risen and glorified Savior at the right hand of the majesty in the heavens.''[2]

4:25 The Lord Jesus ''was delivered for our offenses, and was raised again for our justification.'' Although the preposition ''for'' (Greek *dia*) is used here in connection with both our offenses and our justification, the context demands a different shade of meaning in each case. He was delivered up for our offenses—that is, not only because of them but in order to put them away. He was raised for our justification—that is, in order to demonstrate God's complete satisfaction with the work of Christ by which we are justified. In the first instance, our offenses were the problem that needed to be dealt with. In the second instance, our justification is the result that is assured by Christ's resurrection. There could have been no justification if Christ had remained in the tomb. But the fact that He rose tells us that the work is finished, the price has been paid, and God is infinitely satisfied with the sin-atoning work of the Savior.

CHAPTER 5

The apostle carries his case for justification forward another step by taking up the question: *What are the benefits of justification in the believer's life?* In other words, does it really work? His answer is a resounding *yes,* as he enumerates seven major blessings that every believer possesses. These blessings flow to the believer through the Lord Jesus Christ; He is the Mediator between God and man, and all God's gifts are channeled through Him.

5:1 The first great benefit enjoyed by those of us who have been justified by faith is *peace with God* through our Lord Jesus Christ. The war is over. Hostilities have ceased. Through the work of Christ all causes of enmity between our souls and God have been removed. We have been changed from foes to friends by a miracle of grace. (Many ancient authorities read "let us have peace with God" instead of "we have peace with God." But the sense of the passage demands a statement of fact rather than an exhortation. A copyist probably made the unjustified change.)

5:2 We also enjoy *access into an indescribable position of favor with God.* We are accepted in the Beloved One; therefore we are as near to God and as dear to God as His own Beloved Son. The Father extends the golden scepter to us and welcomes us as sons, not strangers. This grace, or standing in favor, embraces every aspect of our position before God, a position that is as perfect and permanent as Christ's because we are in Him.

As if that were not enough, *we also exult in hope of the glory of God.* This means that we joyfully look forward to the time when we will not only gaze upon the splendor of God, but will ourselves be manifested in glory (see John 17:22; Colossians 3:4). We cannot comprehend the full significance of that hope here on earth, nor will we get over the wonder of it through all eternity.

5:3 The fourth blessing that flows from justification is that *we rejoice in our tribulations*—not so much in their present discomforts as in their eventual results (see Hebrews 12:11). It is one of the delightful paradoxes of the Christian faith that joy can coexist with affliction. The opposite of joy is sin, not suffering. One of the great benefits of tribulation is that it produces endurance or steadfastness. We could never develop endurance if our lives were trouble-free.

5:4 That is what is meant by the statement that endurance works experience (or better, approvedness). When God sees us bearing up under our trials and looking to Him to work out His purposes through them, He awards us His Good Endurance Seal of Approval. We have been tested and approved.

And this sense of His approval fills us with hope. We know He is working in our lives, developing our character. This gives us confidence that, having begun a good work in us, He will see it through to completion (Philippians 1:6).

5:5 "Hope maketh not ashamed." If we were to hope for something but then later find that we were never going to get it, our hope would be put to shame or disappointed. But the hope of our salvation will never be put to shame. We will never be disappointed or find that we have rested on a false confidence.

How can we be so sure? Because the love of God is shed abroad in our hearts. "The love of God" could mean either our love for God or His love for us. Here we know it means the latter because verses 6-20 rehearse some of the great proofs of God's love for us.

The Holy Spirit, given to us the moment we believe, floods our hearts with these expressions of God's eternal love, and by these we are assured that He will see us safely home to heaven.

"One of the things you sense for the first time after you receive the Spirit is that God loves you. I don't mean a vague, misty feeling that Someone somewhere cares about the human race, but an undeniable conviction that a personal God actually *loves you* on a one-to-one basis.''[1]

5:6 In verses 6-20, Paul argues from the lesser to the greater. His logic is that if God's love went out to us when we were His ungodly enemies, will He not much more preserve us now that we belong to Him? This brings us to the fifth benefit of our justification: *we are eternally secure in Christ*. In developing this theme, the apostle introduces five "much mores."

The "much more" of deliverance from wrath (5:9).

The "much more" of preservation by his resurrection life (5:10).

The "much more" of the gift of grace (5:15).

The "much more" of the believer's reign in life (5:17).

The "much more" of abounding grace (5:20).

In verses 6, 7 and 8 Paul emphasizes what we were (without strength, ungodly, sinners) when Christ died for us. In verses 9 and 10 he emphasizes what we are now (justified by Christ's blood, reconciled by His death) and the resulting certainty of what the Savior will do for us (deliver us from wrath, preserve us by His life).

First we are reminded that we were weak, helpless, without strength, and unable to save ourselves, but at the predetermined time the Lord Jesus Christ visited our planet and died for men. And he died not just for good men, as some might suppose, but for the ungodly. There was no virtue, no excellence in us to commend us to God. We were utterly unworthy, but Christ died for us anyway.

5:7 This act of divine love was unique and unparalleled by anything in human experience. The average man's life is precious to him, and he would not think of throwing it away for an unworthy person. For example, he would not die for a murderer, an adulterer, or a mobster. In fact, he would be reluctant to die even for a "righteous" man, one who is honest and dependable but not especially warmhearted. It is possible, in an extreme case, that he would die for a ''good'' man, meaning one who is kind, friendly, loving, and lovable.

5:8 The love of God is completely supernatural and otherworldly. He demonstrated His marvelous love to us by sending His beloved Son to die for us while we were sinners. If we ask why He did it, we must look for the answer in the sovereign will of God Himself. There was no good in us to call forth such love.

5:9 Now a new set of conditions exists. We are no longer reckoned as guilty sinners. At the enormous cost of the Savior's blood, shed for us at Calvary, we have been counted righteous by God. Since He went to such tremendous cost to justify us when we were sinners, will He not much more save us from wrath through Christ? If He has already paid the greatest price to bring us into His favor, is it likely that He would allow us to perish in the end?

The expression ''saved from wrath'' could mean either ''saved out of wrath'' or ''delivered from any contact with wrath.'' Here we believe that the preposition (Greek *apo*) means the latter—saved away from any contact with the wrath of God, either in time or in eternity.

5:10 Going back to what we were and what we now are, think of it this way. It was when we were enemies that we were reconciled to God by the death of His Son. We were hostile toward the Lord and quite content to have it so. Left to ourselves, we felt no need of being reconciled to Him. Think of it—enemies of God!

God did not share our attitude in the matter. He intervened in a display of pure grace. The substitutionary death of Christ removed the cause of our hostility toward God—namely, our sins. By faith in Christ we have been reconciled to God.

If God purchased our reconciliation so dearly, will He ever let us go? If we were reconciled through the death of His Son, which is a symbol of utter weakness, shall we not be preserved to the end by the present life of Christ at the right hand of God, a life of infinite power? If His death had such power to save us, how much more will His life have power to keep us?

We can sing with J. Denham Smith:

> And this I shall find,
> For such is His mind,
> He'll not be in glory
> And leave me behind.

5:11 And now we come to the sixth benefit of justification: *"We rejoice in God through our Lord Jesus Christ"* (RSV). We not only rejoice in His gifts but in the Giver Himself. Before we were saved we found our joys elsewhere. Now we exult whenever we remember Him, and are sad only when we forget Him.

What has produced this marvelous change, so that we can now joy in God? It is the work of the Lord Jesus Christ. Like all our other blessings, this joy comes to us through Him.

The seventh benefit enjoyed by the justified is found in the words *"We have now received the reconciliation"* (NASB). Reconciliation refers to the establishment of harmony between God and man through the sacrificial work of the Savior. The entrance of sin had brought estrangement, alienation, and enmity between man and God. By putting away sin, which had caused the alienation, the Lord Jesus restored those who believe on Him to a state of harmony with God. We should note, in passing, that *God* did not need to be reconciled. It was *man* who needed it, because he was at enmity with God.

The King James Version incorrectly translates this clause "We have now received the atonement." In the strict Old Testament sense, the word *atonement* means *covering*. Sins were covered by the sacrifices but were not put away. However, the word *atonement* is generally used today to describe the work of Christ in satisfying the righteous claims of God, putting away our sins once for all, and giving the assurance that God will never remember them again. This acquired meaning is thus equivalent to *propitiation*. But the Greek word used here in 5:11 is not the word for *propitiation* but rather the one for *reconciliation*.

5:12 The rest of the chapter serves as a bridge between the first part of the letter and the next three chapters. It is linked with the first part by picking up the subjects of condemnation through

Adam and justification through Christ, and by showing that the work of Christ far outweighs in blessing what the work of Adam did in misery and loss. It is linked with chapters 6 through 8 by moving from justification to sanctification, and from acts of sin to sin in human nature.

Adam is portrayed in these verses as the federal head or representative of all those who are in the old creation. Christ is presented as the Federal Head of all those who are in the new creation. A federal head acts for all those who are under him. For example, when the President of a country signs a bill into law, he is acting for all the citizens of that country.

That is what happened in Adam's case. As a result of his sin, human death entered the world. Death became the common lot of all Adam's descendants because they had all sinned in him. It is true that they all committed individual acts of sin as well, but that is not the thought here. Paul's point is that Adam's sin was a *representative act,* and all his posterity are reckoned as having sinned in him.

Someone might object that it was Eve and not Adam who committed the first sin on earth. That is true, but since Adam was the first to be created, *headship* was given to him. So he is seen as acting for all his descendants.

When the Apostle Paul says here in 5:12 that "death passed upon all men," he is referring to *physical* death, even though Adam's sin brought spiritual death as well. (Verses 13 and 14 show that physical death is in view.)

When we come to this passage of Scripture, certain questions inevitably arise. Is it fair that Adam's posterity should be constituted sinners just because he sinned? Does God condemn men for being born sinners, or only for those sins which they have actually committed? If men are born with a sinful nature, and if they therefore sin because they are born sinners, how can God hold them responsible for what they do?

Bible scholars have wrestled with these and a host of similar problems and have come up with a surprising variety of conclusions. However, there are certain facts that we can be sure of.

First, the Bible does teach that all men are sinners, both by nature and by practice. Everyone born of human parents inherits Adam's sin, and also sins by his own deliberate choice.

Second, we know that the wages of sin is death—both physical death and eternal separation from God.

But no one has to pay the penalty of sin unless he wants to. This is the important point. At enormous cost, God sent His Son to die as a Substitute for sinners. Salvation from sin and its wages is offered as a free gift through faith in the Lord Jesus Christ.

Man is condemned on three grounds. He has a sinful nature, Adam's sin is imputed to him, and he is a sinner by practice. But his crowning guilt is his rejection of the provision which God has made for his salvation (John 3:18,19,36).

But someone will ask, "What about those who have never heard the gospel?" This question is answered in part, at least, in chapter 1. Beyond that we can rest in the assurance that the Judge of all the earth will do what is right (Genesis 18:25). He will never act unjustly or unfairly. All his decisions are based on equity and righteousness. Although certain situations pose problems to our dim sight, they are not problems to Him. When the last case has been heard and the doors of the courtroom swing shut, no one will have a legitimate basis for appealing the verdict.

5:13 Paul will now demonstrate that Adam's sin affected the whole race. He first points out that sin was in the world during the period from Adam to the giving of the law at Mount Sinai. But during that time there was no clearly revealed law of God. Adam had received a clear oral commandment from the Lord, and many centuries later the Ten Commandments were a distinct written revelation of divine law. But in the intervening period men did not have a legal code from God. Therefore, although there was sin during that time, there was no transgression, because transgression is the violation of a known law. And sin is not imputed *as transgression* when there is no law forbidding it.

5:14 Yet death did not take a holiday during the age when there was no law. With the single exception of Enoch, death held sway over all mankind. You could not say that these people died because they had transgressed a clear command of God, as Adam did. Why then did they die? The answer is implied: they died because they had sinned in Adam.

If this seems unfair, let us remember that this has nothing to do with the subject of salvation. All those who put their faith in the Lord were saved eternally. But they died *physically* just the same, and the reason they died was because of the sin of their federal head, Adam.

In his role as federal head, Adam was a type (symbol) of Him who was to come—that is, the Lord Jesus Christ. In the succeeding verses Paul will develop the subject of these two federal heads, but more by contrast than by similarities. He will show that—

> In Christ the sons of Adam boast
> More blessings than their father lost

5:15 The first contrast is between the trespass of Adam and the free gift of Christ. By the trespass of the first man, the many died. "The many" here refers, of course, to Adam's descendants. Death here may include spiritual as well as physical death.

The free gift abounds much more unto the many. The free gift is the marvelous manifestation of the grace of God abounding to a race of sinners. It is made possible by the grace of the one Man, the Lord Jesus Christ. It was amazing grace on His part to die for His rebellious creatures. Through His sacrificial death, the gift of eternal life is offered to the many.

The two *manys* in this verse are not coextensive; that is, they do not refer to the same people. The first *many* includes all those who became subject to death as a result of Adam's trespass. The second time the word is used, it means all who become members of the new creation, of which Christ is the Federal Head. It includes only those to whom God's grace has abounded—that is, true believers. While God's mercy is showered on all, His grace is appropriated only by those who trust the Savior.

5:16 There is another important contrast between Adam's sin and Christ's gift. The one sin of Adam brought inevitable judgment, and the verdict was "Condemned." The free gift of Christ, on the other hand, dealt effectively with many offenses, not just one, and resulted in the verdict "Acquitted." Paul highlights the differences between Adam's sin and Christ's gift, between the terrible havoc wrought by one sin and the tremendous deliverance wrought from many sins, and finally between the verdict of condemnation and the verdict of acquittal.

5:17 By the one trespass of one man, death reigned as a cruel tyrant. But by the gracious gift of righteousness, a gift of overflowing grace, all believers reign in life through the Lord Jesus Christ.

What grace this is! We are not only delivered from death's reign as a tyrant over us, but we reign as kings, enjoying life now and eternally. Do we really understand and appreciate this? Do we live as the royalty of heaven, or do we grovel among the muckheaps of this world?

5:18 The offense of Adam brought condemnation to all men, but the righteousness of Christ brought justification of life to all. Here the righteousness of Christ does not mean His righteousness as a Man on earth or His perfect keeping of the law. These are never said to be imputed to us. If they were, then it would not have been necessary for Christ to die. The New American Standard Bible is on target when it translates: "So then as through one transgression there resulted condemnation to all men, even so through one act of righteousness there resulted justification of life to all men." The "one act of righteousness" was not the Savior's life or His keeping of the law, but rather His substitutionary death on Calvary's Cross. This is what brought justification of life—that is, the justification that results in life—and brought it to all men.

The two "alls" in this verse do not refer to the same people. The first "all" means all who are in Adam. The second "all" means all who are in Christ. This is clear from the words in the preceding verse "they which *receive* abundance of grace and the gift of righteousness. . . ." *The gift must be received by faith.* Only those who trust the Lord receive justification of life.

5:19 Just as by Adam's disobedience to God's command many were made sinners, so by Christ's obedience to the Father's will the many who trust Him are declared righteous. Christ's obedience led Him to the Cross as our Sinbearer.

It is futile for universalists to use these verses to try to prove that all men will eventually be saved. The passage deals with two federal headships, and it is clear that just as Adam's sin affects those who are ''in him,'' so Christ's righteous act benefits only those who are ''in Him.''

5:20 What Paul has been saying would come as a jolt to the Jewish objector who felt that everything revolved around the law. Now this objector learns that sin and salvation center not in the law but in two federal heads. That being the case, he might be tempted to ask, ''Why then was the law given?'' The apostle answers, ''The law came in by the way so that the offense might abound.'' It did not originate sin, but it revealed sin as an offense against God. It did not save from sin but revealed sin in all its awful character.

But God's grace proves to be greater than all man's sin. Where sin abounded, God's grace at Calvary abounded more exceedingly!

5:21 Now that the reign of sin, inflicting death on all men, has been ended, grace reigns in righteousness, giving eternal life through Jesus Christ our Lord. Notice that grace reigns in *righteousness*. All the demands of God's holiness have been met, and the penalty of the law has been paid, so God can now grant eternal life to all who come pleading the merits of Christ, their Substitute.

Perhaps we have in these verses a partial answer to the familiar question, ''Why did God allow sin to enter the world?'' The answer is that God has received more glory and man has received more blessings through Christ's sacrifice than if sin had never entered. We are better off in Christ than we ever could have been in an unfallen Adam.

If Adam had never sinned, he would have enjoyed continued life on earth in the Garden of Eden. But he had no prospect of becoming a redeemed child of God, an heir of God, or a joint-heir with Jesus Christ. He had no promise of a home in heaven or of being with Christ and like Him forever. These blessings come only through the redemptive work of the Lord Jesus Christ.

CHAPTER 6

What Paul had said at the close of chapter 5—that grace superabounded over all man's sin—raises another question, and a very important one. *Does the teaching of the gospel (salvation by grace through faith) encourage or even permit sinful living?*

The answer, an emphatic denial, extends over chapters 6 through 8. Here in chapter 6 the answer centers around three key words: KNOW (vv. 3,6), RECKON or CONSIDER (v. 11), and YIELD or PRESENT (v. 13).

It will help us to follow Paul's argument in this chapter if we understand the difference between the believer's position and his practice. His position is his standing in Christ. His practice is what he is or should be in everyday life.

Grace puts us into the position, then teaches us to walk worthy of it. Our position is absolutely perfect because we are *in Christ*. Our practice should increasingly correspond to our position. It never will correspond perfectly until we see the Savior in heaven, but we should be becoming more and more conformed to His image in the meantime.

The apostle first sets forth the truth of our identification with Christ in death and resurrection, and then exhorts us to live in the light of this great truth.

6:1 The Jewish objector comes forward with what he thinks is a clinching argument. If the gospel of grace teaches that man's sin provides for an even greater display of God's grace, then doesn't it suggest that we should continue in sin that grace might be magnified all the more?

65

A modern version of this argument is as follows: "You say that men are saved by grace through faith, apart from the law. But if all you have to do to be saved is believe, then you could go out and live in sin." According to this argument, grace is not a sufficient motivation for holy living. You must put people under the restraints of the law.

It has been helpfully suggested that there are four answers in the chapter to the initial question, "Shall we continue in sin?"

     a) You CANNOT, because you are united to Christ.
          Reasoning (vv. 1-11)
     b) You NEED NOT, because sin's dominion has been broken by grace.
          Appealing (vv. 12-14)
     c) You MUST NOT, because it would bring sin in again as your master.
          Commanding (vv. 15-19)
     d) You HAD BETTER NOT, for it would end in disaster.
          Warning (vv. 20-23)[1]

6:2 Paul's first answer, then, is that we cannot continue in sin because we have died to it. This is a positional truth. When Jesus died to sin, He died as our Representative. He died not only as our *Substitute*—that is, *for* us or *in our place*—but He also died as our *Representative*—that is, *as* us. Therefore, when He died, we died. He died to the whole question of sin, settling it once and for all. All those who are in Christ are seen by God as having died to sin.

This does not mean that the believer is sinless. It means that he is identified with Christ in His death, and in all that His death means.

6:3 The first key word in Paul's presentation is KNOW. Here he introduces the subject of baptism to show that it is morally incongruous for believers to go on in sin. But the question immediately arises, "To which baptism is he referring?" So an introductory word of explanation is necessary.

When a person is saved, he is baptized unto Christ Jesus in the sense that he is identified with Christ in His death and resurrection. This is not the same as the baptism in (or of) the Spirit, though both occur simultaneously. The latter baptism places the believer in the body of Christ (1 Corinthians 12:13); it is not a baptism unto death. The baptism unto Christ means that in the reckoning of God, the believer has died with Christ and has risen with Him.

When Paul speaks of baptism here, he is thinking both of our spiritual identification with Christ and of its portrayal in water baptism. But as the argument advances, he seems to shift his emphasis in a special way to water baptism as he reminds his readers how they were ''buried'' and ''planted together'' in the ''likeness'' of Christ's death.

The New Testament never contemplates the abnormal situation of an unbaptized believer. It assumes that those who are converted submit to baptism right away. Thus our Lord could speak of faith and baptism in the same breath: ''he that believeth and is baptized shall be saved'' (Mark 16:16). Though baptism is not a requirement for salvation, it should be the invariable public sign of it.

6:4 Water baptism gives a visual demonstration of baptism unto Christ. It pictures the believer being immersed in death's dark waters (in the person of the Lord Jesus), and it pictures the new man in Christ rising to walk in newness of life. There is a sense in which a believer attends the funeral of his old self when he is baptized. As he goes under the water he is saying, ''All that I was as a sinful son of Adam was put to death at the Cross.'' As he comes up out of the water he is saying, ''Nevertheless I live; yet not I, but Christ liveth in me'' (see Galatians 2:20).

The apostle moves on to state that the resurrection of Christ makes it possible for us to walk in newness of life. He states that our Lord Jesus Christ was raised from the dead by the glory of the Father. This simply means that all the divine perfections of God—His righteousness, His love, His justice, etc.—demanded that He raise the Lord. In view of the excellence of the Person of the

Savior, it would not have been consistent with God's character to leave the Savior in the tomb.

God did raise Him, and because we are identified with Christ in His resurrection, we can and should walk in newness of life.

> The Lord is ris'n; with Him we also rose,
> And in His grave see vanquished all our foes.
> The Lord is ris'n: beyond the judgment land,
> In Him, in resurrection-life we stand.
>
> —William P. Mackay

6:5 Just as we have been united with Christ in the likeness of His death, we shall also be united with Him in the likeness of His resurrection. The words "the likeness of his death" refer to the believer's being put under the water in baptism. The actual union with Christ in His death took place nearly 2000 years ago, but baptism is a "likeness" of what happened then.

We not only go under the water; we come up out of the water, a "likeness" of His resurrection. While it is true that the phrase "in the likeness" is not part of the original text in the second part of this verse, it must be supplied to complete the meaning.

Just as we have been united with Christ in the likeness of His death (immersion in water), so we are united with Him in the likeness of His resurrection (being raised out of the water). The clause "we shall be" does not necessarily indicate futurity. Hodge says, "The reference is not to what is to happen hereafter, but to the certainty of sequence, or causal connection. If the one thing happens, the other shall surely follow."

6:6 We confess in baptism that our old man was crucified with Christ. Our old man refers to all that we were as children of Adam—our old, evil, unregenerate selves, with all our old habits and appetites. At conversion we put off the old man and put on the new man, as if exchanging filthy rags for spotless clothing (Colossians 3:9,10).

The crucifixion of the old man at Calvary means that the body of sin has been put out of commission. The body of sin does not refer to the physical body. Rather, it means indwelling sin, personified as a tyrant, ruling the person. This body of sin is not "destroyed" (RSV) or "done away with" (NASB) but is *annulled* or *rendered inoperative as a controlling power*. The last clause shows that this is the meaning: "that we should no longer be slaves to sin" (NIV). The tyranny of sin over us has been broken.

6:7 When a man dies, he is justified from sin (ASV). Here is a man, for example, who is sentenced to die in the electric chair for murdering a police officer. As soon as he dies, he is justified from that sin. The penalty has been paid and the case is closed.

Now we have died with Christ on the Cross of Calvary. Not only has our penalty been paid, but sin's stranglehold on our lives has been broken. We are no longer the helpless captives of sin.

6:8 Our death with Christ is one side of the truth. The other side is that we shall also live with Him. We have died to sin; we live unto righteousness. Sin's dominion over us has been shattered; we share Christ's resurrection life here and now. And we shall share it for all eternity, praise His Name!

6:9 Our confidence is based on the fact that the risen Christ will never die again. Death has no more dominion over Him. Death did have dominion over Him for three days and nights, but that dominion is forever passed. Christ can never die again!

6:10 When the Lord Jesus died, He died to the whole subject of sin once for all. He died to sin's claims, its wages, its demands, its penalty. He finished the work and settled the account so perfectly that it never needs to be repeated.

Now that He lives, He lives unto God. In one sense, of course, He always lived to God. But now He lives to God in a new relationship, as the Risen One, and in a new sphere, where sin can never enter.

Before going on, let us review what we have learned in the first ten verses. The general subject is sanctification—God's method for holy living. As to our standing before God, we are seen as having died with Christ and having risen with Him. This is pictured in baptism. Our death with Christ ends our history as men and women in Adam. God's sentence on our old man was not reformation but death. And that sentence was carried out when we died with Christ. Now we are risen with Christ to walk in newness of life. Sin's tyranny over us has been broken, because sin has nothing to say to a dead person. Now we are free to live unto God.

6:11 Paul has described what is true of us *positionally*. Now he turns to the *practical outworking* of this truth in our lives. We are to RECKON ourselves to be dead unto sin but alive unto God in Christ Jesus.

To "reckon" here means to accept what God says about us as true and to live in the light of it. It means "believing what God says in Romans 6:6 and knowing it as a fact in one's own personal salvation. This demands a definite act of faith, which results in a fixed attitude toward 'the old man.' We will see him where God sees him—on the Cross, put to death with Christ. Faith will operate continuously to keep him where grace placed him. This involves us very deeply, for it means that our hearty consent has been given to God's condemnation of and judgment upon that old 'I' as altogether unworthy to live and as wholly stripped of any further claims upon us. The first step in a walk of practical holiness is this reckoning upon the crucifixion of 'the old man.' "[2]

We reckon ourselves dead to sin when we respond to temptation as a dead man would. One day Augustine was accosted by a woman who had been his mistress before his conversion. When he turned and walked away quickly, she called after him, "Augustine, it's me! it's me!" Quickening his pace, he called back over his shoulder, "Yes, I know, but it's no longer me."[3]

What he meant was that he was dead to sin and alive to God. A dead man has nothing to do with immorality, lying, cheating, gossiping, or any other sin.

Now we are alive to God in Christ Jesus. This means that we are called to holiness, worship, prayer, service, and fruitbearing.

6:12 We saw in 6:6 that our old man was crucified so that sin as a reigning tyrant might be knocked out, so that we would no longer be the helpless captives of sin. Now the practical exhortation is based on what is true positionally. We should not let sin reign in our mortal bodies by obeying its evil desires. At Calvary the reign of sin was ended by death. Now we must make it so practically. Our cooperation is needed. Only God can make us holy, but He will not do it without our willing involvement.

6:13 That brings us to the third key word in this chapter—YIELD. We must not yield the members of our body to sin, to be used as weapons or tools of wickedness. Our obligation is to turn control of our members to God, to be used in the cause of righteousness. After all, we have been raised to life from death; and, as we were reminded in 6:4, we should walk in newness of life.

6:14 Now another reason is given why sin will not have dominion over us as believers. The first reason was that our old man was crucified with Christ (6:6). The second reason is that we are not under law but under grace.

Sin does have the upper hand over a person who is under law. Why? Because the law tells him what to do but doesn't give him the power to do it. And the law stirs up dormant desires in fallen human nature to do what is forbidden. It's the old story that "forbidden fruit is sweet."

Sin does not have dominion over the man who is under grace. The believer has died to sin. He has received the indwelling Holy Spirit as the power for holy living. And he is motivated by love for the Savior, not by fear of punishment. Grace is the only thing that really produces holiness. As Denney put it, "It is not restraint but inspiration that liberates from sin; not Mount Sinai but Mount Calvary which makes saints."[4]

6:15 Those who are afraid of grace insist that it gives license for sinning. Paul meets this error head-on by asking the question, then flatly denying it. We are free from the law but not lawless. Grace means freedom to serve the Lord, not to sin against Him.

In 6:1 the question was, "Shall we continue in sin?" Here the question is, "Shall we sin just a little?" The answer in both cases is a horrified "No!"

6:16 It is a simple fact of life that when we submit ourselves to someone as our master we become that person's servant. Likewise, if we sell out to sin, we become slaves of sin, and eternal death lies waiting at the end of that road. If, on the other hand, we choose to obey God, the result is a holy life. Sin's slaves are bound by guilt, fear, and misery, but God's servants are free to do what the new nature loves. So why be a slave when you can be free?

6:17 "Thank God that you, who were at one time the servants of sin, honestly responded to the impact of Christ's teaching when you came under its influence" (Phillips). The Roman Christians had given wholehearted obedience to the gospel of grace to which they had been committed, including all the doctrines which Paul has been teaching in this letter.

6:18 Correct doctrine should lead to correct duty. Responding to the truth that they had been made free from sin as master, they became bondslaves of righteousness.

The phrase "free from sin" does not mean that they no longer had a sinful nature. Neither does it mean that they no longer committed acts of sin. The context shows that it is referring to freedom from sin as the dominating power in their life.

6:19 In the previous verse the apostle had spoken of bondslaves of righteousness, but he realizes that those who live righteously are not actually in bondage. "Practical righteousness is not slavery, except when we speak after the manner of men."[5] Those who practice sin are the bondslaves of sin, but those whom the Son sets free are free indeed (John 8:34,36).

Paul explains that, in using the simile of slaves and master, he is speaking after the manner of men; that is, he is using a familiar illustration from everyday life. He does this because of the weakness of their flesh—in other words, because of their intellectual and spiritual difficulty in understanding truth when it is stated in general terms. Truth often needs to be illustrated in order to become intelligible.

Before their conversion the believers had surrendered their

bodies as slaves to all kinds of impurity and to one kind of wickedness after another. Now they should dedicate those same bodies as slaves of righteousness, so that their lives would be truly holy.

6:20 When they were in bondage to sin, the only freedom they knew was freedom from righteousness. It was a desperate condition to be in—bound by every evil and free from every good.

6:21 Paul challenges them (and us) to inventory the fruits of an unsaved life, fruits in those activities which now bring shame to a believer. Marcus Rainsford has drawn up such an inventory, as follows: "1. Faculties abused. 2. Affections prostrated. 3. Time squandered. 4. Influence misused. 5. Best friends wronged. 6. Our best interests violated. 7. Love outraged—especially the love of God. Or to sum it up in one word—SHAME."[6]

The end of those things is death. "Every sin tends to death, and, if persisted in, ends in death as its goal and fruit."[7]

6:22 Conversion changes a man's position completely. Now he is free from sin as his master, and he becomes a willing servant to God. The result is a holy life now and eternal life at the end of the journey. Of course the believer has eternal life now too, but this verse refers to that life in its fullness, including the glorified resurrection body.

6:23 The apostle summarizes the subject by presenting these vivid contrasts:

Two masters—sin and God.

Two methods—wages and free gift.

Two aftermaths—death and eternal life.

Notice that eternal life is in a Person, and that Person is the Lord Jesus Christ. All who are in Christ have eternal life. It's as simple as that!

CHAPTER 7

The apostle now anticipates a question that will inevitably arise: *What is the relationship of the Christian to the law?* Perhaps Paul had Jewish believers especially in mind in answering this question, since the law was given to the nation of Israel, but the principles apply just as much to Gentile believers who foolishly want to put themselves under the law as a rule of life after they have been justified.

In the previous chapter we saw that death ended the tyranny of the sin nature in the life of the child of God. Now we will see that death likewise ends the dominion of the law over those who were under it.

7:1 This verse is connected with 6:14: "You are not under law, but under grace" (NASB). The connection is, "You should know that you are not under law—or are you ignorant of the fact that the law has dominion over a man only when he is alive?" Paul is speaking to those who are familiar with fundamental principles of law, and who therefore should know that the law has nothing to say to a dead man.

7:2 To illustrate this, Paul shows how death breaks the marriage contract. A woman is bound by the marriage law to her husband as long as he is alive. But if he dies, she is discharged from that law.

7:3 If a woman is married to another man while her husband is living, she is guilty of adultery. If, however, her husband dies, she is free to marry again without any cloud or guilt of wrongdoing.

74

7:4 In applying the illustration, we must not press each detail with exact literalness. For example, neither the husband nor the wife represents the law. The point of the illustration is that just as death breaks the marriage relationship, so the death of the believer with Christ breaks the jurisdiction of the law over him.

Notice that Paul does not say that the law is dead. The law still has a valid ministry in producing conviction of sin. And remember that when he says "we" in this passage, he is thinking of those who were Jews before they came to Christ.

We have been made dead to the law by the body of Christ, the body here referring to the giving up of His body in death. We are no longer joined to the law; we are now joined to the risen Christ. One marriage has been broken by death, and a new one has been formed. And now that we are free from the law, we can bring forth fruit unto God.

7:5 This mention of fruit brings to mind the kind of fruit we brought forth when we were in the flesh. The expression "in the flesh" obviously doesn't mean "in the body." "In the flesh" here is descriptive of our standing before we were saved. Then the flesh was the basis of our standing before God. We depended on what we were or what we could do to win acceptance with God. "In the flesh" is the opposite of "in Christ."

Prior to our conversion we were ruled by sinful passions which were stimulated by the law. It is not that the law originated them, but only that by naming them and then forbidding them it stirred up the strong desire to do them.

These passions of sin found expression in our physical members, and when we yielded to temptation we brought forth poison fruit that results in death. Elsewhere the apostle speaks of this fruit as the works of the flesh—immorality, impurity, sensuality, idolatry, sorcery, enmities, strife, jealousy, outbursts of anger, disputes, dissensions, factions, envyings, drunkenness, and carousings (Galatians 5:19-21 NASB).

7:6 Among the many wonderful things that happen when we are converted is that we are discharged from the law. This is a result of our having died with Christ. Since He died as our Representative, we died with Him. In His death He fulfilled all the claims of the law by paying its awful penalty. Therefore we are free from the law and from its inevitable curse. There can be no double jeopardy.

> Payment God will not twice demand—
> First at my bleeding Surety's hand
> And then again at mine.
>
> —Augustus M. Toplady

The words in the King James Version "that being dead wherein we were held" incorrectly imply that the law that held us is dead. But the law is not dead; rather, we are dead to the law. This is indicated in the wording of the New American Standard Bible: "having died to that by which we were bound."

We are now set free to serve in newness of the spirit and not in oldness of the letter. Our service is motivated by love, not fear; it is a service of freedom, not bondage. It is no longer a question of slavishly adhering to minute details of forms and ceremonies but of the joyful outpouring of ourselves for the glory of God and the blessing of others.

7:7 It might seem from all this that Paul is critical of the law. He had said that believers are dead to sin and dead to the law, and this might have created the impression that the law is evil. But this is far from the case.

In 7:7-13 he goes on to describe the important role which the law played in his own life before he was saved. He emphasizes that the law itself is not sinful, but that it *reveals sin in man*. It was the law that convicted him of the terrible depravity of his heart. As long as he compared himself with other people, he felt fairly respectable. But as soon as the demands of God's law came home to him in convicting power, he stood speechless and condemned.

The one particular commandment that revealed his sin to him was the tenth: "Thou shalt not covet." Coveting takes place in the mind. Although Paul may not have committed any of the grosser, more revolting sins, he now realized that his thought life was corrupt. He understood that evil thoughts are sinful as well as evil deeds. He had a polluted thought life. His outward life may have been relatively blameless, but his inward life was a chamber of horrors.

7:8 "Sin, taking occasion by the commandment, wrought in me all manner of concupiscence." The word translated "concupiscence" means "coveting." When the law forbids all kinds of evil coveting, man's corrupt nature is inflamed all the more to do it. For example, the law says, in effect, "You must not conjure up all sorts of pleasurable sexual encounters in your mind. You must not live in a world of lustful fantasies." The law forbids a dirty, vile, suggestive thought-life. But unfortunately it doesn't give the power to overcome. So the result is that man under law becomes more involved in a dreamworld of sexual uncleanness than he ever was before. He comes to realize that whenever an act is forbidden, his fallen nature wants to do it all the more. "Stolen waters are sweet, and bread eaten in secret is pleasant" (Proverbs 9:17).

Apart from the law sin is dead, relatively speaking. The sinful nature is like a sleeping dog. When the law comes and says "Don't," the dog wakes up and goes on a rampage, doing excessively whatever is forbidden.

7:9 Before being convicted by the law Paul was alive; that is, his sinful nature was *comparatively* dormant and he was blissfully ignorant of the pit of iniquity in his heart.

But when the law came—that is, when it came with crushing conviction—his sinful nature became thoroughly inflamed. The more he tried to obey, the worse he failed.

He died as far as any hope of achieving salvation by his own character or efforts was concerned. He died to any thought of his own inherent goodness. He died to any dream of being justified by law-keeping.

7:10 He found that the commandment which was unto life actually turned out to be unto death for him. But what does he mean that the commandment was "unto life" (ASV)? This probably looks back to Leviticus 18:5, where God said, "So you shall keep My statutes and My judgments, by which a man may live if he does them; I am the Lord" (NASB). *Ideally* the law promised life to those who kept it. *Actually* no sinful son of Adam could keep it. The sign outside a lion's cage says, "Stay back of the railing." If obeyed, the commandment is unto life. But for the child who disobeys and reaches in to pet the lion, it is unto death.

7:11 Once again the apostle emphasizes that the law was not to blame. It was indwelling sin that incited him to do what the law prohibited. Sin tricked him into thinking that the forbidden fruit wasn't so bad after all, that it would bring him happiness, and that he could get away with it. It suggested that God was withholding pleasures from him that were for his good.

Thus sin slew him in the sense that it spelled death to his best hopes of deserving or earning salvation.

7:12 The law itself is holy, and each commandment is holy, righteous, and good. In our thinking we must constantly remember that there is nothing wrong with the law. It was given by God and therefore is perfect as an expression of His will for His people. The weakness of the law lay in the "raw materials" it had to work with: it was given to people who were already sinners. They needed the law to give them the knowledge of sin, but beyond that they needed a Savior to deliver them from the penalty and power of sin.

7:13 "That which is good" in this verse refers to the law, as is specifically stated in the preceding verse. Paul raises the question "Did the law become death to me," which means "Is the law the culprit, dooming Paul (and all the rest of us) to death?" The answer, of course, is "No! *Sin* is the culprit." The law didn't originate sin, but it showed sin in all its exceeding sinfulness. "By the law is the knowledge of sin" (3:20b). But that is not all! How does man's sinful nature respond when God's holy law forbids it to do something? The answer is well-known. What may have been a dormant desire now becomes a burning passion. Thus through the commandment sin becomes exceedingly sinful.

There might seem to be a contradiction between what Paul says here and in 7:10. There he said he found the law to be unto death. Here he denies that the law became death to him. The solution is this. The law by itself can neither improve the old nature on the one hand nor cause it to sin on the other. It can reveal sin, just as a thermometer reveals the temperature. But it cannot *control* sin like a thermostat controls the temperature.

But what happens is this. Man's fallen human nature instinctively wants to do whatever it is forbidden to do. So it uses the law to awaken otherwise-dormant lusts in the life of the sinner. The more man tries, the worse it gets, till at last he is brought to despair of hope. Thus sin uses the law to cause any hope of improvement to die in him. And he sees the exceeding sinfulness of his old nature as he never saw it before.

7:14 Up to this point the apostle has been describing a past experience in his life—namely, the traumatic crisis when he underwent deep conviction of sin through the law's ministry.

Now he changes to the present tense to describe an experience he had since he was born again—namely, the conflict between the two natures and the impossibility of finding deliverance from the power of indwelling sin through his own strength.

Paul acknowledges that the law is spiritual—that is, holy in itself and adapted to man's spiritual benefit. But he realizes that he is carnal because he is not experiencing victory over the power of indwelling sin in his life. He is sold under sin. He feels as if he is sold as a slave with sin as his master.

7:15 Now the apostle describes the struggle that goes on in a believer who does not know the truth of his identification with Christ in death and resurrection. It is the conflict between the two natures in the person who climbs Mount Sinai in search of holiness. "Here was a man trying to achieve holiness by personal effort, struggling with all his might to fulfill God's 'holy and righteous and good' commandments (v. 12), only to discover that the more he struggled, the worse his condition became. It was a losing battle, and no wonder, for it is not in the power of fallen human nature to conquer sin and live in holiness."[1]

You will notice the prominence of the first-person pronouns—I, me, my, myself; they occur over 40 times in verses 9-25! People who go through this Romans 7 experience have taken an overdose of Vitamin "I." They are introspective to the core, searching for victory in self, where it cannot be found.

Incidentally, most of modern Christian psychological counseling focuses the counselee's attention upon himself and thus adds to the problem instead of relieving it. People need to know that they have died with Christ and have risen with Him to walk in newness of life. Then, instead of trying to improve the flesh, they will relegate it to the grave of Jesus.

In describing the struggle between the two natures, Paul says, "I do not understand my own actions" (RSV). He is a split personality, a Dr. Jekyll and Mr. Hyde. He finds himself indulging in things that he doesn't want to do, and practicing things that he hates.

7:16 In thus committing acts which his better judgment condemns, he is taking sides with the law against himself, because the law condemns them too. So he gives inward assent that the law is right.

7:17 This leads to the conclusion that the culprit is not the new man in Christ, but the sinful, corrupt nature that dwells in him. But we must be careful here. We must not excuse our sinning by passing it off to indwelling sin. *We* are responsible for what we do, and we must not use this verse to "pass the buck." All Paul is doing here is tracking down the source of his sinful behavior, not excusing it.

7:18 There can be no progress in holiness until we learn what Paul learned here—that in me (that is, in my flesh) dwells no good thing. The flesh here means the evil, corrupt nature which is inherited from Adam and which is still in every believer. It is the source of every evil action which a person performs. There is nothing good in it.

When we learn this, it delivers us from ever looking for any good in the old nature. It delivers us from being disappointed when we don't find any good there. And it delivers us from occupation with ourselves. There is no victory in introspection. As the saintly McCheyne said, for every look we take at ourselves, we should take ten looks at Christ.

To confirm the hopelessness of the flesh, the apostle mourns that although he has the desire to do what is right, he doesn't have the resources in himself to translate his desire into action. The trouble, of course, is that he is casting his anchor inside the boat.

7:19 Thus the conflict between the two natures rages on. He finds himself failing to do the good things he wants to do, and instead doing the evil that he despises. He is just one great mass of contradictions and paradoxes.

7:20 We might paraphrase this verse as follows: "Now if I (the old nature) do that which I (the new nature) do not want to do, it is no more I (the person) who does it, but sin that dwells within me." Again let it be clear that Paul is not excusing himself or disclaiming responsibility. He is simply stating that he has not found deliverance from the power of indwelling sin, and that when he sins, it is not with the desire of the new man.

7:21 He finds a principle or law at work in his life causing all his good intentions to end in failure. When he wants to do what is right, he ends up by sinning.

7:22 As far as his new nature is concerned, he delights in the law of God. He knows that the law is holy, and that it is an expression of the will of God. He wants to do God's will.

7:23 But he sees a contrary principle at work in his life, striving against the new nature, and making him a captive of indwelling sin.

"The law, though he delights in it after the inward man, gives him no power. In other words, he is trying to accomplish what God has declared to be an utter impossibility—namely, making the flesh subject to God's holy law. He finds that the flesh minds the things of the flesh, and is very enmity itself to the law of God, and even to God Himself.''[2]

7:24 Now Paul lets out his famous, eloquent groan. He feels as if he has a decomposing body strapped to his back. That body, of course, is the old nature in all its corruption.

In his wretchedness he acknowledges that he is unable to deliver himself from this offensive, repulsive bondage. He must have help from some outside source.

7:25 The burst of thanksgiving which opens this verse may be understood in at least two ways. It may mean "I thank God that deliverance comes through Jesus Christ our Lord" or it may be an aside in which Paul thanks God through the Lord Jesus that he is no longer the wretched man of the preceding verse.

The rest of the verse summarizes the conflict between the two natures before deliverance is realized. With the renewed mind, or the new nature, the believer serves the law of God, but with the flesh or old nature the law of sin. Not till we reach the next chapter do we find the way of deliverance explained.

CHAPTER 8

The subject of holy living continues. In chapter 6 Paul had answered the question, "Does the teaching of the gospel (salvation by faith alone) encourage or even permit sinful living?" In chapter 7 he faced up to the question, "Does the gospel tell Christians to keep the law in order to lead a holy life?" Now the question is: *How is the Christian enabled to live a holy life?*

We notice right away that the personal pronouns that were so prominent in chapter 7 largely disappear, and that the Holy Spirit becomes the dominant Person. This is an important key to understanding the passage. Victory is not in ourselves but in the Holy Spirit, who indwells us.

8:1 From the valley of despair and defeat, the apostle now climbs the heights with the triumphant shout, "There is therefore now no condemnation to those who are in Christ Jesus!" This may be understood in two ways.

First, there is no divine condemnation as far as our sin is concerned, because we are in Christ. There was condemnation as long as we were in our first federal head, Adam. But now we are in Christ and therefore are as free from condemnation as He is. So we can hurl out the challenge:

> Reach my blest Savior first,
> Take Him from God's esteem;
> Prove Jesus bears one spot of sin,
> Then tell me I'm unclean.
>
> —W. N. Tomkins

But it may also mean that there is no need for the kind of self-condemnation which Paul described in the preceding chapter. We may pass through a Romans 7 experience, unable to fulfill the law's requirements by our own effort, but we don't have to stay there. The following verse explains why there is no condemnation.

(Incidentally, the last part of this verse in the KJV should be omitted. The words "who walk not after the flesh but after the Spirit" are not supported by the best manuscript authorities or by the sense of the passage. They properly belong where they are found, at the end of verse 4.)

8:2 It is the Spirit's law of life in Christ Jesus that has made us free from the law of sin and death. These are two opposite laws or principles. The characteristic principle of the Holy Spirit is to empower believers for holy living. The characteristic principle of indwelling sin is to drag a person down to death. It is like the law of gravity. When you throw a baseball into the air, it comes back down because it is heavier than the air it displaces. A living bird is also heavier than the air it displaces, but when you toss it up in the air, it flies away. The law of life in the bird overcomes the law of gravity. So the Holy Spirit supplies the risen life of the Lord Jesus, making the believer free from the law of sin and death.

8:3 The law could never get men to fulfill its sacred requirements, but grace has succeeded where law failed. Let us see how!

The law could not produce holy living because it was weak through the flesh. The trouble was not with the law but with fallen human nature. The law spoke to men who were already sinners and who were without strength to obey.

But God intervened by sending His own Son in the likeness of sinful flesh. Take careful notice that the Lord Jesus did not come in sinful flesh itself but in *the likeness of* sinful flesh. He did no sin (1 Peter 2:22), He knew no sin (2 Corinthians 5:21), and there was no sin in Him (1 John 3:5). But by coming into the world in human form, He resembled sinful humanity.

As a sacrifice for sin, Christ condemned sin in the flesh. He died not only for the sins which we commit (1 Peter 3:18) but also for our sin nature. In other words, He died for what we *are* just as much as for what we have *done*. In so doing, He condemned sin in the flesh. Our sin nature is never said to be forgiven; it is condemned. It is the sins that we have *committed* that are forgiven.

8:4 Now the righteous requirements of the law are fulfilled in us who walk not after the flesh but after the Spirit. As we turn over the control of our lives to the Holy Spirit, He empowers us to love God and to love our neighbor, and that, after all, is what the law requires.

We should pause here to point out that in these first four verses the apostle has gathered together the threads of his argument from 5:12 to 7:25. In 5:12-21 he had discussed the federal headships of Adam and of Christ. Now in 8:1 he shows that the condemnation which we inherited from our identification with Adam is removed by our identification with Christ. In chapters 6 and 7 he discussed the horrendous problem of sin in the nature. Now he announces triumphantly that the Spirit's law of life in Christ Jesus has made us free from the law of sin and death. In chapter 7 the whole subject of the law was brought up. Now we learn that the law's requirements are met by the Spirit-controlled life.

8:5 Those who are after the flesh—that is, those who are unconverted—are concerned with the things of the flesh. They obey the impulses of the flesh. They live to gratify the desires of the corrupt nature. They cater to the body, which in a few short years will return to dust.

Those who are after the Spirit—that is, true believers—rise above flesh and blood and live for those things that are eternal. They are occupied with the Word of God, with prayer, with worship, and with Christian service.

8:6 The mind of the flesh—that is, the mental inclination of the fallen nature—is death. It is death as far as both present enjoyment and ultimate destiny are concerned. It has all the potential of death in it, just like an overdose of poison.

The mind of the Spirit is life and peace. The Spirit of God is the guarantee of life that is life indeed, of peace with God, and of a life of tranquility.

8:7 The reason why the mind-set of the flesh is death is because it is enmity against God. The sinner is a rebel against God and in active hostility to Him. If any proof were needed, it is seen most clearly in the crucifixion of the Lord Jesus Christ.

The mind of the flesh is not subject to the law of God. It wants its own will, not God's will. It wants to be its own master, not to bow to His rule.

Its nature is such that it cannot be subject to God's law. It is not only the *inclination* that is missing but the *power* as well. The flesh is dead toward God.

8:8 It is no surprise, therefore, that those who are in the flesh cannot please God. Think of that! There is nothing an unsaved person can do to please God—no good works, no religious observances, no sacrificial services, absolutely nothing. First he must take the guilty sinner's place and receive Christ by a definite act of faith. Only then can He win God's smile of approval.

8:9 When a person is born again, he is no longer in the flesh but in the Spirit. He lives in a different realm and in a different sphere. Just as a fish lives in water and physical man lives in the air, so the believer lives in the Spirit.

He not only lives in the Spirit, but the Spirit lives in him. In fact, if he is not indwelt by the Spirit of Christ, he does not belong to Christ. Though there is a question whether the Spirit of Christ here is the same as the Holy Spirit, the assumption that they are the same seems to fit best in the context.

8:10 Through the ministry of the Spirit, Christ is actually in the believer. It is amazing to think of the Lord of life and glory dwelling in our bodies, especially when we remember that these bodies are subject to death because of sin. Someone may argue that they are not dead yet, as the verse seems to say. No, but the forces of death are already working in them, and they will inevitably die if the Lord doesn't return in the meantime.

In contrast to the body, the spirit is life because of righteousness. Though once dead toward God, it has been made alive through the righteous work of the Lord Jesus Christ in His death and resurrection, and because the righteousness of God has been credited to our account.

8:11 But the reminder that the body is still subject to death need cause no alarm or despair. The fact that the Holy Spirit indwells our bodies is a guarantee that, just as He raised the Lord Jesus from the dead, so He will give life to our mortal bodies. This will be the final act of our redemption—when our bodies are glorified like the Savior's body of glory.

8:12 Now when we see the stark contrast between the flesh and the Spirit, what conclusion do we draw? We owe nothing to the flesh to live according to its dictates. The old, evil, corrupt nature has been nothing but a drag. It has never done us a bit of good. If Christ had not saved us, the flesh would have dragged us down to the deepest, darkest, hottest places in hell. Why should we feel obligated to such an enemy?

8:13 Those who live after the flesh must die, not only physically but eternally. To live after the flesh is to be unsaved. This is made clear in 8:4,5.

But why does Paul address this to those who were already Christians? Does he imply that some of them might eventually be lost? No, but the apostle often includes words of warning and self-examination in his letters, realizing that in every congregation there may be some people who have never been genuinely born again.

The rest of the verse describes what is characteristically true of genuine believers. By the enablement of the Holy Spirit they put to death the deeds of the body. They enjoy eternal life now, and will enter into life in its fullness when they leave this earth.

8:14 Another way of describing true believers is to say that they are led by the Spirit of God. Paul is not referring here to spectacular instances of divine guidance in the lives of eminent Christians. Rather, he is speaking of what is true of all the sons of God—namely, that they are led by the Spirit of God. It is not a question of the degree in which they are yielded to the Holy Spirit, but of a relationship which takes place at the time of conversion.

Sonship implies reception into God's family, with all the privileges and responsibilities of adult sons. A new convert does not have to wait a certain time before he enters into his spiritual inheritance; it is his the moment he is saved, and it applies to all believers, both men and women.

8:16 Those living under law are like minor children, bossed around as if they were servants, and shadowed by the fear of punishment.

But when a person is born again, he is not born into a position of servitude. He is not brought into God's household as a slave. Rather, he receives the spirit of adoption; that is, he is placed in God's family as a mature son. By a true spiritual instinct he looks up to God and calls Him Abba, Father. Abba is an Aramaic word which suffers in translation. It is an intimate, familiar form of the word *father*—such as "papa" or "dad." While we may hesitate to use such familiar English words in addressing God, the truth remains that He who is infinitely high is also intimately nigh.

The phrase "the spirit of adoption" may be a reference to the Holy Spirit as the One who makes the believer aware of his special dignity as a son. Or it may mean the realization or attitude of adoption in contrast to the spirit of bondage.

"Adoption" is used in three different ways in this epistle. Here it refers to the consciousness of sonship which the Holy Spirit produces in the life of the believer. In 8:23 it looks forward to that time when the believer's body will be redeemed or glorified. In 9:4 it looks back to that time when God designated Israel as His son (Exodus 4:22).

In two other occurrences in the New Testament, Galatians 4:5 and Ephesians 1:5, the word means "son-placing"—that is, the act of placing all believers as mature, adult sons with all the privileges and responsibilities of sonship. Every believer is a child of God in that he is born into a family of which God is the Father. But every believer is also a son—a special relationship carrying the privileges of one who has reached the maturity of manhood.

"Adoption" in the New Testament never means what it means in our society—to take a child of other parents as one's own.

8:16 As mentioned above, there is a spiritual instinct in the new-born believer that he is a son of God. The Spirit tells him that it is so. The Holy Spirit also bears witness with the believer's spirit that he is a member of God's family. How does the Holy Spirit do this? Primarily it is through the Word of God. As a Christian reads the Bible, the Spirit confirms the truth that, because he has trusted the Savior, he is now a child of God.

The phrase "the Spirit itself" (KJV) should read "the Spirit Himself" (NASB). The Holy Spirit is a Person, not an influence. While the Greek word *pneuma,* meaning wind, breath, and spirit, is neuter, it should always be used in the masculine gender when referring to the Holy Spirit.

8:17 Membership in God's family brings privileges that boggle the mind. All God's children are heirs of God. An heir, of course, eventually inherits his father's estate. That is just what is meant here. All that the Father has is ours. We have not yet come into the possession and enjoyment of all of it, but nothing can prevent our doing so in the future.

And we are joint-heirs with Christ. When He returns to take the scepter of universal government, we will share with Him the title deeds to all the Father's wealth.

When Paul adds, "if so be that we suffer with Him, that we may be also glorified together," he is not making heroic suffering a condition for salvation. Neither is he describing some elite inner circle of overcomers who have endured great afflictions. Rather, he sees all Christians as being cosufferers and all Christians as glorified with Christ. The "if" is equivalent to "since."

Of course, there are some who suffer more than others in the cause of Christ, and this will result in differing degrees of reward and of glory. But all who acknowledge Jesus as Lord and Savior are seen here as incurring the hostility of the world, with all its shame and reproach.

8:18 The greatest shame that we may endure for Christ here on earth will be a mere trifle when He calls us forth and publicly acknowledges us before the hosts of heaven. Even the excruciating pain of the martyrs will seem like pinpricks when the Savior graces their brows with the crown of life. Elsewhere Paul speaks of our present sufferings as light afflictions which are only for a moment, but he describes the glory as an exceeding and eternal weight (2 Corinthians 4:17). Whenever he describes the coming glory, his words seem to bend under the weight of the idea. If we could only appreciate the glory that is to be ours, we would count the sufferings along the way as trivia!

8:19 Now in a bold literary figure the apostle personifies the whole creation as eagerly looking forward to the time when we will be revealed to a wondering world as the sons of God. This will be when the Lord Jesus Christ returns to reign and we return with Him.

We are already the sons of God, but the world neither recognizes nor appreciates us as such. And yet the world is looking forward to a better day, and that day cannot come till the King returns to reign with all His saints.

8:20 When Adam sinned, his transgression affected not only mankind, but all creation, both animate and inanimate. The ground is cursed. Many wild animals die violent deaths. Disease afflicts birds and animals as well as fish and serpents. The results of man's sin have rippled like shockwaves throughout all creation.

Thus, as Paul explains, the creation was not plunged into futility, frustration, and disorder by its own choice, but by the decree of God because of the disobedience of man's first federal head.

The words "in hope" at the end of this verse should probably be connected with the following verse: "in hope that the creation also itself shall be delivered . . ." (see ASV).

8:21 Creation looks back to the ideal conditions that existed in Eden. Then it surveys the havoc that was caused by the entrance of sin. Always there has been the hope of a return to an idyllic state, when creation will be delivered from the bondage of corruption to enjoy the freedom of that golden era when we as God's children will be revealed in glory.

8:22 We live in a sighing, sobbing, suffering world. All creation groans and suffers pain like that of childbirth. Nature's music is in the minor key. The earth is wracked by cataclysm. The blight of death is on every living thing.

8:23 Believers are not exempt. Although they have the firstfruits of the Spirit, guaranteeing their eventual deliverance, they still groan for that day of glory.

The Holy Spirit is the firstfruits. Just as the first handful of ripened grain is a pledge of the entire harvest to follow, so the Holy Spirit is the pledge or guarantee that the full inheritance will be ours.

Specifically, He is the guarantee of the coming adoption, the redemption of the body (Ephesians 1:14). In one sense we have already been adopted, which means that we have been placed into God's family as sons. But in a fuller sense our adoption will be complete when we receive our glorified bodies. That is spoken of as the redemption of our bodies. Our spirits and souls have already been redeemed, and our bodies will be redeemed at the time of the Rapture (1 Thessalonians 4:13-18).

8:24 We were saved by hope—that is, in this attitude of hope. We did not receive all the benefits of our salvation at the moment of conversion. From the outset we looked forward to full and final deliverance from sin, suffering, disease, and death.

If we had already received these blessings, we wouldn't be hoping for them. We only hope for what is in the future.

8:25 Our hope for deliverance from the presence of sin and all its baneful results is based on the promise of God, and is therefore as certain as if we had already received it. So we wait for it with patience and steadfastness.

8:26 Just as we are sustained by this glorious hope, so we are sustained by the Holy Spirit in our infirmities. We are often perplexed in our prayer life. We don't know how to pray as we should. We pray selfishly, ignorantly, narrowly. But once again the Spirit comes alongside to assist us in our weakness, interceding with us with groanings which cannot find expression. In this verse it is the Spirit who groans and not we who groan, though that is also true.

There is mystery here. We are peering into the unseen, spiritual realm where a great Person and great forces are at work on our behalf. And although we cannot understand it all, we can take infinite encouragement from the fact that a groan may sometimes be the most spiritual prayer.

8:27 If God can search the hearts of men, He can also interpret the mind of the Spirit, even though that mind finds expression only in groans. The important thing is that the Holy Spirit's prayers for us are always in accordance with the will of God. And because they are always in accordance with God's will, they are always for our good. That explains a lot, as the next verse goes on to show.

8:28 God is working all things together for good to those who love Him, to those who are called according to His purpose. It might not always seem so. Sometimes when we are suffering heartbreak, tragedy, disappointment, frustration, and bereavement, we wonder what good can come out of it. But the following verse gives the answer: whatever God permits to come into our lives is designed to conform us to the image of His Son. When we see this, it takes the question mark out of our prayers.

Some ancient authorities read ''God worketh all things with them for good'' instead of ''All things work together for good.'' In other words, our lives are not controlled by impersonal forces such as chance or luck but by our wonderful, personal Lord, who is ''too loving to be unkind and too wise to err.''

8:29 Now Paul traces the majestic sweep of the divine program designed to bring many sons to glory.

First of all, God foreknew us in eternity past. This was not a mere intellectual knowledge. As far as knowledge is concerned, He knew everyone who would ever be born. But His foreknowledge embraced only those whom He foreordained or predestinated to be conformed to the image of His Son. So it was knowledge with a purpose that could never be frustrated.

It is not enough to say that God foreknew those whom He realized would one day repent and believe. Actually it is His foreknowledge that insures eventual repentance and belief.

That ungodly sinners should one day be transformed into the image of Christ by a miracle of grace is one of the most astounding truths of divine revelation. The point is not, of course, that we will ever have the attributes of deity, or even that we will have Christ's facial resemblance, but that we will be *morally* like Him, absolutely free from sin, and will have glorified bodies like His.

In that day of glory He will be the Firstborn among many brethren. Firstborn here means first in rank or honor. He will not be One among equals, but the One who has the supreme place of honor among His brothers.

8:30 Everyone who was predestinated in eternity is called in time. This means that he not only hears the gospel but that he responds to it as well. It is therefore an effectual call. All are called; that is the general (and genuine) call of God. But only a few respond; that is the effectual (conversion-producing) call of God.

All who respond are justified or given an absolutely righteous standing before God. They are clothed with the righteousness of God through the merits of Christ and are thereby fit for the presence of the Lord.

Those who are justified are also glorified. Actually we are not glorified as yet, but it is so sure that God can use the past tense in describing it. We are as certain of the glorified state as if we had already received it.

This, incidentally, is one of the strongest passages in the

New Testament on the eternal security of the believer. For every million people who are foreknown and predestinated by God, every one of that million will be called, justified, and glorified. Not one will be missing.

8:31 When we consider these unbreakable links in the chain of our redemption, the conclusion is inevitable! If God is for us, in the sense that He has marked us out for Himself, then no one can be successful against us. If Omnipotence is working on our behalf, no lesser power can defeat His program.

8:32 "He who spared not His own Son, but delivered Him up for us all. . . ." What marvelous words! We must never allow our familiarity with them to dull their luster or lessen their power to inspire worship. When a world of lost mankind needed to be saved by a sinless Substitute, the great God of the universe did not hold back His heart's best Treasure, but gave Him over to a death of shame and loss on our behalf.

The logic that flows from this is irresistible. If God has already given us the greatest gift, is there any lesser gift that He will not give? If He has already paid the highest price, will He hesitate to pay any lower price? If He has gone to such lengths to procure our salvation, will He ever let us go? "How shall He not with Him also freely give us all things?"

"The language of unbelief is, 'How shall He?' The language of faith is 'How shall He not?' "[1]

8:33 We are still in a courtroom setting, but now a remarkable change has taken place. While the justified sinner stands before the bench, the call goes out for any accusers to step forward. But there is none! How can there be? If God has already justified His elect, who can bring a charge?

It greatly clarifies the argument of this verse and the following one if we supply the words "No one because . . ." before each answer. Thus this verse would read, "Who shall lay anything to the charge of God's elect? *No one because* it is God who justifies." If we do not supply these words, it might sound as if God is going to lay something to the charge of His elect, and that is the very thing that Paul is denying.

8:34 Another challenge rings out! Is there anyone here to condemn? *No one because* Christ has died for the defendant, has been raised from the dead, is now at God's right hand interceding for him. If the Lord Jesus, to whom all judgment has been committed, does not pass sentence on the defendant but rather prays for him, then there is no one else who could have a valid reason for condemning him.

8:35 Now faith flings its final challenge: is there anyone here who can banish the justified from the love of Christ? A search is made for every adverse circumstance that has been effective in causing separations in other areas of human life. But none can be found. Not the threshing flail of tribulation with its steady pounding of distress and affliction, nor the monster of anguish, bringing extreme pain to mind and body, nor the brutality of persecution, inflicting suffering and death on those who dare to differ. Nor can the gaunt specter of starvation—gnawing, racking, and wasting down to the skeleton. Nor can nakedness, with all that it means in the way of privation, exposure, and defenselessness. Nor can peril—the threat of imminent and awful danger. Nor can the sword—cold, hard, and death-dealing.

8:36 If any of these things could separate the believer from the love of Christ, then the fatal severance would have taken place long ago, because the career of the Christian is a living death. That is what the psalmist meant when he said that, because of our identification with the Lord, we are killed throughout the day, and are like sheep that are doomed to slaughter (Psalm 44:22).

8:37 Instead of separating us from Christ's love, these things only succeed in drawing us closer to Him. We are not only victors, but more than victors. It is not simply that we triumph over these formidable forces, but that in doing so we bring glory to God, blessing to others, and good to ourselves. We make slaves out of our enemies and stepping stones out of our roadblocks.

But all of this is not through our own strength, but only through the One who loved us. Only the power of Christ can bring sweetness out of bitterness, strength out of weakness, triumph out of tragedy, and blessing out of heartbreak.

8:38 The apostle has not finished his search. He ransacks the universe for something that might conceivably separate us from God's love, then dismisses the possibilities one by one—

death with all its terrors;

life with all its allurements;

angels and principalities, supernatural in power and knowledge;

things present, crashing in upon us;

things to come, arousing fearful forebodings;

powers, whether human tyrants or angelic adversaries;

8:39 heights or depths, those things that are in the realm of dimension or space.

Then, to make sure that he is not missing anything, Paul adds:

"anything else in all creation" (RSV).

The outcome of Paul's search is that he can find nothing that can separate us from the love of God, which is in Christ Jesus our Lord.

No wonder these words of triumph have been the song of those who have died martyr's deaths and the rhapsody of those who have lived martyr's lives!

CHAPTER 9

In chapters 9 through 11 we hear Paul's answer to the Jewish objector who asks: *Does the gospel, by promising salvation to Gentiles as well as Jews, mean that God has broken His promises to His earthly people, the Jews?* Paul's answer covers Israel's past (chapter 9), its present (chapter 10), and its future (chapter 11).

You will notice that this section contains a great emphasis on divine sovereignty and human responsibility. Romans 9 is one of the key passages in the Bible on the sovereign election of God. The next chapter sets forth the balancing truth—the responsibility of man—with equal vigor.

When we say that God is sovereign, we mean that He is in charge of the universe and that He can do as He pleases. In saying that, however, we know that, because He is God, He will never do anything that is wrong, unfair, or unrighteous. Therefore, to say that God is sovereign is merely to allow God to be God. We should not be afraid of this truth or apologize for it. It is a glorious truth and should cause us to be worshipers.

In His sovereignty, God has elected or chosen certain individuals to belong to Himself. But the same Bible that teaches God's sovereign election also teaches human responsibility. While it is true that God elects men to salvation, it is also true that men must choose to be saved by a definite act of the will. The divine side of salvation is seen in the words, "All that the Father giveth me shall come to me." The human side is found in the words that follow: "and him that cometh to me I will in no wise

97

cast out'' (John 6:37). We rejoice, as believers, that God chose us in Christ before the foundation of the world (Ephesians 1:4). But we believe just as surely that whosoever will may take of the water of life freely (Revelation 22:17). Someone has illustrated the two truths this way: when we come to the door of salvation, we see the invitation overhead, ''Whosoever will may come.'' When we pass through, we look back and see the words ''Elect according to the foreknowledge of God'' above the door. Thus the truth of man's responsibility faces men as they come to the door of salvation. The truth of sovereign election is a family secret for those who have already entered.

How can it be that God chooses individuals to belong to Himself and at the same time makes a bona fide offer of salvation to all men everywhere? How can we reconcile these two truths? The fact is that we cannot reconcile them. To the human mind they are in conflict. But the Bible teaches both doctrines, and so we should believe them, content to know that the difficulty lies in our minds and not in God's. These twin truths are like two parallel lines that meet only in infinity.

Some have tried to reconcile sovereign election and human responsibility by saying that God foreknew who would trust the Savior and that those are the ones whom He elected to be saved. They base this on Romans 8:29 (''whom He did foreknow He also did predestinate'') and 1 Peter 1:2 (''elect according to the fore-knowledge of God''). But this overlooks the fact that God's fore-knowledge is *determinative*. It is not just that He *knows* in advance who will trust the Savior, but that He *predetermines* this result by drawing certain individuals to Himself.

Although God chooses some men to be saved, He never chooses anyone to be damned. To put it another way, though the Bible teaches election, it never teaches divine reprobation. But someone may object, ''If God elects some to blessing, then He necessarily elects others to destruction.'' But that is not true! The whole human race was doomed to destruction by its own sin and not by any arbitrary decree of God. If God allowed everyone to go to hell—and He could justly have done that—men would be getting exactly what they deserved. The question is, ''Does the sovereign Lord have a right to stoop down and select a handful of otherwise-doomed people to be a bride for His Son?'' The answer, of course, is that He does have this right. So what it boils down to is this: if men are lost, it is because of their own sin and rebellion; if men are saved, it is because of the sovereign, electing grace of God.

To the man who is saved, the subject of God's sovereign choice should be the cause of unceasing wonder. The believer looks around and sees people with better characters and better personalities and better dispositions than his own, and asks, ''Why did the Lord choose me?''

> Why was I made to hear Thy voice,
> And enter while there's room,
> When thousands make a wretched choice,
> And rather starve than come?
>
> —Isaac Watts

The truth of election should not be used by the unsaved for excusing their unbelief. They must not say, ''If I'm not elect, there's nothing I can do about it.'' The only way they can ever know they are elect is by repenting of their sins and receiving Jesus Christ as Lord and Savior (1 Thessalonians 1:4-7).

Neither should the truth of election be used by Christians to excuse a lack of evangelistic zeal. We must not say, ''If they're elect, they'll be saved anyway.'' Only God knows who the elect are. We are commanded to preach the gospel to all the world, for God's offer of salvation is a genuine invitation to all people. People reject the gospel because of the hardness of their hearts, and not because God's universal invitation is insincere.

There are two dangers to be avoided in connection with this subject. The first is to hold only one side of the truth—for example, to believe in God's sovereign election and to deny that a man has any responsible choice in connection with his salvation. The other danger is to overemphasize one truth at the expense of the other. The scriptural approach is to believe in God's sovereign election and to believe with equal force in human responsibility. Only in this way can a person hold these doctrines in their proper biblical balance.

Now let us turn to Romans 9 and follow the beloved apostle as he unfolds this subject.

9:1 In insisting that salvation is for Gentiles as well as for Jews, Paul gave the appearance of being a traitor, a turncoat, a renegade as far as Israel was concerned. So he here protests his deep devotion to the Jewish people by using a solemn oath. He speaks the truth. He is not lying. His conscience, in fellowship with the Holy Spirit, attests the truth of what he is saying.

9:2 When he thinks first of Israel's glorious calling, and now of its rejection by God because of its rejection of the Messiah, his heart is filled with great sorrow and continual anguish.

9:3 He could even wish himself accursed or cut off from Christ if through the forfeiting of his own salvation his Jewish brothers might be saved. In this strong statement of self-abnegation, we sense the highest form of human love—that which constrains a man to lay down his life for his friends (John 15:13). And we feel the enormous burden which a converted Jew experiences for the conversion of his kinsmen. It reminds us of Moses' prayer for his people: "Yet now, if Thou wilt forgive their sin—and if not, blot me, I pray Thee, out of Thy book which thou hast written" (Exodus 32:32).

9:4 As Paul weeps over his people, their glorious privileges pass in review. They are Israelites, members of God's ancient chosen people.

God had adopted that nation to be His son (Exodus 4:22) and delivered His people out of Egypt (Hosea 11:1). He was a father to Israel (Deuteronomy 14:1), and Ephraim was his firstborn (Jeremiah 31:9). (*Ephraim* is used here as another name for the nation of Israel.)

The Shekinah or glory cloud symbolized God's presence in their midst, guiding and protecting them.

It was with Israel, not with the Gentiles, that God made the covenants. It was with Israel, for example, that He made the Palestinian Covenant, promising them the land from the River of Egypt to the Euphrates (Genesis 15:18). And it is with Israel that

He will yet ratify the New Covenant, promising ''the perpetuity, future conversion, and blessing of a repentant Israel (Jeremiah 31:31-40).''[1]

It was to Israel that the law was given. They and they alone were its recipients.

The elaborate rituals and services connected with the tabernacle and the temple were given to Israel, as well as the priesthood.

In addition to the covenants mentioned above, God made innumerable promises to Israel of protection, peace, and prosperity.

9:5 The Jewish people rightfully claim the patriarchs as their own—Abraham, Isaac, Jacob, and the 12 sons of Jacob. These were the forefathers of the nation. And they had the greatest privilege of all—the Messiah is an Israelite, as far as His human descent is concerned, though He is also the Sovereign of the universe, God blessed for ever. Here we have a positive statement of the deity and humanity of the Savior. (Some Bible versions weaken the force of this verse. For example, the Revised Standard Version reads, ''. . . and of their race, according to the flesh, is the Christ. God who is over all be blessed for ever. Amen.'' The Greek does not decide which translation is correct, but spiritual discernment in comparing Scripture with Scripture accepts the reading in the King James Version and other conservative translations.)

9:6 The apostle now faces up to a serious theological problem. If God made promises to Israel as His chosen earthly people, how can this be squared with Israel's present rejection and with the Gentiles being brought into the place of blessing?

Paul insists that this does not indicate any breach of promise on God's part. He goes on to show that God has always had a sovereign selection process based upon promise and not just on lineal descent.

Just because a person is born into the nation of Israel does not mean that he is an heir to the promises. Within the nation of Israel, God has a true, believing remnant.

9:7 Not all Abraham's offspring are counted as his children. Ishmael, for example, was of the seed of Abraham. But the line of promise came through Isaac, not through Ishmael. The promise of God was "In Isaac shall thy seed be called" (Genesis 21:12). As we pointed out in the notes on 4:12, the Lord Jesus made this same interesting distinction when talking with the unbelieving Jews in John 8:33-39. They said to Him, "We are Abraham's seed . . ." (v. 33). Jesus admitted this, saying, "I know you are Abraham's seed" (v. 37). But when they said, "Abraham is our father," the Lord replied, "If you were Abraham's children, you would do the works of Abraham" (v. 39). In other words, they were descended from Abraham, but they didn't have Abraham's faith and therefore they were not his spiritual children.

9:8 We see from this that it is not physical descent that counts. The true Israel consists of those Jews who were selected by God and to whom He made some specific promise, marking them out as His children. We see this principle of sovereign election in the cases of Isaac and Jacob.

9:9 God appeared to Abraham, promising that He would return at the appointed time and that Sarah would have a son. That son, of course, was Isaac. He was truly a child of promise and a child of supernatural birth.

9:10 Another case of sovereign election is found in the case of Jacob. Isaac and Rebecca were the parents, of course. But Rebecca was carrying two babies, not one.

9:11 A pronouncement was made before the children were ever born. This pronouncement could not, therefore, have had anything to do with works of merit by either child. It was entirely a matter of God's choice, based on His own will and not on the character or attainments of the subjects. The purpose of God according to election means His determination to distribute His favors according to His sovereign will and good pleasure.

This verse, incidentally, disproves the idea that God's choice of Jacob was based on His foreknowledge of what Jacob would do. It specifically says that it was not made on the basis of works.

9:12 The decision was that the elder would serve the younger. Esau would have a subservient place to Jacob. It was not a question of being chosen to *eternal life* but to *earthly glory and privilege.*

Esau was the firstborn of the twin brothers and ordinarily would have had the honors and privileges associated with that position. But God's selection passed him by and rested on Jacob.

9:13 To further enforce God's sovereignty in choosing, Paul quotes Malachi 1:2,3: "I loved Jacob, and I hated Esau." Here God is speaking of the two nations, Israel and Edom, of which Jacob and Esau were heads. God marked out Israel as the nation to whom He promised the Messiah and the messianic kingdom. Edom received no such promise. Instead, its mountains and heritage were laid waste for the dragons of the wilderness (Malachi 1:3; see also Jeremiah 49:17,18; Ezekiel 35:6).

Although it is true that the quotation from Malachi 1:2,3 describes God's dealings with nations rather than individuals, it is used to support His sovereign right to choose individuals as well.

The words "I loved Jacob and I hated Esau" must be understood in the light of the sovereign decree of God that stated, "The elder shall serve the younger." This preference for Jacob is interpreted as an act of love, whereas the bypassing of Esau is seen as hatred by comparison. It is not that God hated Esau with a harsh, vindictive animosity, but only that He loved Esau less than Jacob, as seen by His sovereign selection of Jacob.

This passage refers only to *earthly blessings,* and not to eternal life. God's hatred of Edom doesn't mean that individual Edomites can't be saved, any more than His love of Israel means that individual Jews don't need to be saved. (Note also that Esau did receive some earthly blessings, as he himself testified in Genesis 33:9.)

9:14 The apostle correctly anticipated that his teaching on sovereign election would stir up all kinds of objections. People still accuse God of unfairness. They say that if He chooses some, then He thereby necessarily damns the rest. They argue that if

God has settled everything in advance, then there's nothing man can do about it, and God is unrighteous for condemning man.

Paul hotly denies any possibility of unrighteousness on God's part. But instead of watering down God's sovereignty in order to make it more palatable to these objectors, he proceeds to restate it more vigorously and without apology.

9:15 He first quotes God's word to Moses, "I will have mercy on whom I have mercy, and I will have compassion on whom I have compassion" (see Exodus 33:19). Who can say that the Most High, the Lord of heaven and earth, does not have the right to show mercy and compassion?

All men are condemned by their own sin and unbelief. If left to themselves, they would all perish. In addition to extending a genuine gospel invitation to all men, God chooses some of these condemned men to be special objects of His grace. But this does not mean that He arbitrarily chooses the others to be condemned. They are already condemned because they are lifelong sinners and have rejected the gospel. Those who are chosen can thank God for His grace. Those who are lost have no one to blame but themselves.

9:16 The conclusion, then, is that the ultimate destiny of men or of nations does not rest in the strength of their will or in the power of their exertions, but rather in the mercy of God.

When Paul says that "it is not of him that willeth," he does not mean that a man's will is not involved in his salvation. The gospel invitation is clearly directed to man's will, as shown in Revelation 22:17: "Whosoever will, let him take the water of life freely." Jesus exposed the unbelieving Jews as being *unwilling* to come to Him (John 5:40).

When Paul says, ". . . nor of him that runneth," he does not deny that we must strive to enter the narrow gate (Luke 13:24). A certain amount of spiritual earnestness and willingness are necessary.

But man's will and man's running are not the primary, determining factors: salvation is of the Lord. ". . . No willing on our part, no running of our own, can procure for us the salvation we need, or enable us to enter into the blessings it provides. . . . Of ourselves we shall have no will for salvation, and shall make no effort toward it. Everything of human salvation begins in God.''[2]

9:17 God's sovereignty is seen not only in showing mercy to some but in hardening others. Pharaoh is cited as an example.

There is no suggestion here that the Egyptian monarch was doomed from the time of his birth. What happened was this. In adult life he proved to be wicked, cruel, and extremely stubborn. In spite of the most solemn warnings he kept hardening his heart. God could have destroyed him instantly, but He didn't. Instead, God preserved him alive in order that He might display His power in him, and that through him God's Name might be known worldwide. Here the expression ''raised up'' means ''carefully kept.''

9:18 Pharaoh repeatedly hardened his own heart, and *after* each of these times God *additionally* hardened Pharaoh's heart as a judgment upon him. The same sun that melts ice hardens clay. The same sun that bleaches cloth tans the skin. The same God who shows mercy to the brokenhearted also hardens the impenitent. Grace rejected is grace denied.

God has the right to show mercy to whomever He wishes, and to harden whomever He wishes. But because He is God, He never acts unjustly.

9:19 Paul's insistence on God's right to do what He pleases raises the objection that, if this is so, He shouldn't find fault with anyone, since no one can successfully resist His will. To the objector, man is a helpless pawn on the divine chessboard. Nothing he can do or say will change his fate.

9:20 The apostle first rebukes the insolence of any creature who dares to find fault with his Creator. Finite man, laden with sin, ignorance, and weakness, is in no position to talk back to God or question the wisdom or justice of His ways.

9:21 Then Paul uses the illustration of the potter and the clay to vindicate the sovereignty of God. The potter comes into his shop one day and sees a pile of formless clay on the floor. He picks up a handful of the clay, puts it on his wheel, and fashions a beautiful vessel. Does he have a right to do that?

The Potter, of course, is God. The clay is sinful, lost humanity. If the Potter left it alone, it would all be sent to hell. He would be absolutely just and fair if He left it alone. But instead He extends a bona fide gospel invitation to all men. When all men refuse this invitation, He sovereignly selects a handful among them, saves them by His grace, and conforms them to the image of His Son. Does He have the right to do that? Remember, He is not arbitrarily dooming the others to hell. They are already doomed by their own willfulness and rejection of the gospel.

God has the absolute right and authority to make a vessel of beauty with some of the clay and a vessel of dishonor with some. In a situation where everyone is unworthy, He can bestow His blessings where He chooses and withhold them whenever He wishes. "Where all are undeserving, the utmost that can be demanded is that He should not treat any with injustice."[3]

9:22 Paul pictures God, the great Potter, as facing a seeming conflict of interests. On the one hand, He wishes to display His wrath and exhibit His power in punishing sin. But on the other hand He desires to bear patiently with "vessels of wrath fitted to destruction." It is the contrast between the righteous severity of God in the first place, and His merciful longsuffering in the second. And the argument is, "If God would be justified in punishing the wicked immediately but, instead of that, shows great patience with them, who can find fault with Him?"

We should carefully notice the phrase "vessels of wrath fitted to destruction." Vessels of wrath are those whose sins make them subject to God's wrath. They are fitted to destruction by their own sin, disobedience, and rebellion, and not by some arbitrary decree of God.

9:23 Who can object if God wishes to show the treasures of His glory to people to whom He desires to show mercy—people whom He had previously selected for eternal glory? Here C. R. Erdman's comment seems especially helpful: "God's sovereignty is never exercised in condemning men who ought to be saved, but rather it has resulted in the salvation of men who ought to be lost.''[4]

God does not fit vessels of wrath to destruction, but He does fit vessels of mercy to glory.

9:24 Paul identifies the vessels of mercy as those of us who are Christians, whom God called from both the Jewish and Gentile worlds. This lays the foundation for much that is to follow—the setting aside of all but a remnant of the nation of Israel and the call of the Gentiles to a place of privilege.

9:25 The inspired apostle quotes two verses from Hosea to show that the call of the Gentiles should not have come as a surprise to the Jews. The first is Hosea 2:23: ''I will call them my people which were not my people, and her beloved, which was not beloved.'' Now actually these words in Hosea refer to Israel and not to the Gentiles at all. They look forward to the time when Israel will be restored as God's people and as His beloved. But when Paul quotes them here in Romans he applies them to the call of the Gentiles. What right does Paul have to make such a radical change? The answer is that the Holy Spirit who inspired the words in the first place has the right to reinterpret or reapply them later.

9:26 The second verse in Hosea 1:10: ''And it shall come to pass that in the place where it was said unto them, Ye are not my people, there shall they be called the children of the living God.'' Once again, in its Old Testament setting this verse is not speaking about the Gentiles but is describing Israel's future restoration to God's favor. Yet Paul takes it out of context and applies it to God's acknowledgment of the Gentiles as His sons. This is another illustration of the fact that when the Holy Spirit quotes verses from the Old Testament in the New Testament, He can rightfully apply them as He wishes.

9:27 The rejection of all but a remnant of Israel is discussed in 9:27-29. Isaiah predicted that only a minority of the children of Israel would be saved, even though the nation itself might grow to tremendous numbers (Isaiah 10:22).

9:28 When Isaiah said, ''He will finish the work and cut it short in righteousness'' and ''a short work will the Lord make upon the earth'' (Isaiah 10:23), he was referring to the invasion of Palestine (by the Babylonians) and Israel's subsequent exile. The ''work,'' of course, was God's work of judgment. In quoting these words Paul is saying that what had happened to Israel in the past could and would happen again in his day.

9:29 As Isaiah said before (in an earlier part of his prophecy), Israel would have been wiped out like Sodom and Gomorrah if the Lord of the armies of heaven had not left some survivors (Isaiah 1:9): ''like a small portion of the harvest that is reserved for sowing.''

9:30 What then, Paul asks, is the conclusion of all this as far as this present church age is concerned? The first conclusion is that the Gentiles, who characteristically didn't follow righteousness but rather wickedness, and who certainly didn't pursue a righteousness of their own making, have found righteousness through faith in the Lord Jesus Christ. Not all Gentiles, of course, but only those who believed in Christ were justified.

9:31 Israel, on the other hand, which sought justification on the basis of law-keeping, never found a law by which they might obtain righteousness.

9:32 The reason is clear. They refused to believe that justification is by faith in Christ, but went on stubbornly trying to work out their own righteousness by personal merit. They stumbled over the Stumbling-stone, Christ Jesus the Lord.

9:33 This is exactly what the Lord foretold through Isaiah. The Messiah's coming to Jerusalem would have a twofold effect. To some people He would prove to be a Stumbling-stone and Rock of offense (Isaiah 8:14). Others would believe on Him and find no reason for shame, offense, or disappointment (Isaiah 28:16).

CHAPTER 10

10:1 It is true that Paul's teachings were most distasteful to the unconverted Jews. They considered him a traitor and an enemy of Israel. But here he assures his Christian brethren to whom he was writing that the thing that would bring the greatest delight to his heart and the thing for which he prays to God most earnestly is the salvation of the people of Israel.

10:2 Far from condemning them as godless and irreligious, the apostle gives his testimony that they have a zeal for God. This was apparent from their careful observance of the rituals and ceremonies of Judaism, and from their intolerance of every contrary doctrine. But zeal is not enough; it must be connected with truth. Otherwise it can do more harm than good.

10:3 This is where they failed. They were ignorant of God's righteousness, ignorant of the fact that God imputes righteousness on the principle of faith and not of works. They went about trying to produce a righteousness of their own by law-keeping. They tried to win God's favor by their own efforts, their own character, their own good works. They steadfastly refused to submit to God's plan for reckoning righteous those ungodly sinners who believe on His Son.

10:4 If they had only believed on Christ, they would have seen that He is the end of the law for righteousness. The purpose of the law is to reveal sin, to convict and condemn transgressors. It can never impart righteousness. The penalty of the broken law is death. In His death, Christ paid the penalty of the law which men had broken. When a sinner receives Jesus Christ as his Savior and Lord, the law has nothing more to say to him. Through the death of his Substitute, he has died to the law. He is through with the law and with the futile attempt to achieve righteousness through it.

10:5 In the language of the Old Testament, we can hear the difference between the words of law and the words of faith. In Leviticus 18:5, for example, Moses wrote that the man who achieves the righteousness which the law demands will live by doing so. The emphasis is on his achieving, his doing.

Of course, this statement presents an ideal which no sinful man can meet. All it is saying is that if a man could keep the law perfectly and perpetually, he would not be condemned to death. But the law was given to people who were already sinners and who were already condemned to death. Even if they could keep the law perfectly from that day forward, they still would be lost because God requires payment for those sins which are past. Any hopes that men may have for obtaining righteousness by the law are doomed to failure from the outset.

10:6 In order to show that the language of faith is quite different from that of the law, Paul first quotes from Deuteronomy 30:12,13, which reads:

It is not in heaven, that thou shouldest say,
Who shall go up for us to heaven, and bring it unto us,
that we may hear it and do it?
Neither is it beyond the sea, that thou shouldest say,
Who shall go over the sea for us, and bring it unto us,
that we may hear it and do it?

The interesting thing is that, in their setting in Deuteronomy, these verses are not referring to faith and the gospel at all. They are speaking about the law, and specifically the commandment to "turn unto the Lord thy God with all thine heart and with all thy soul" (Deuteronomy 30:10b). God is saying that the law is not hidden, distant, or inaccessible. A man doesn't have to go up to heaven or cross the sea to find it. It is near at hand and waiting to be obeyed.

But the Apostle Paul takes these words and reapplies them to the gospel. He says that the language of faith doesn't ask a man to climb to heaven to bring Christ down. For one thing, that would be utterly impossible; but it would also be quite unnecessary, because Christ has already come down to earth in His incarnation.

10:7 When the apostle quotes Deuteronomy 30:13, he changes it from ". . . who shall go over the sea" to "who shall descend into the deep," meaning the abyss or the grave. His point is that the gospel does not ask men to descend into the grave to bring Christ up from among the dead. This would be impossible, but it would also be unnecessary, because Christ has already risen from the dead.

Notice that in 10:6,7 we have the two doctrines concerning Christ which were hardest for a Jew to swallow—His incarnation and His resurrection. Yet he must accept these if he is to be saved. We will see these two doctrines again in 10:9,10.

10:8 If the gospel doesn't tell men to do the humanly impossible, or to do what has already been done by the Lord, what then does it say?

Again Paul adapts a verse from Deuteronomy 30 to say that the gospel is near, accessible, intelligible, and easily obtained; it can be expressed in familiar conversation ("in thy mouth"); and it can be readily understood in the mind ("in thy heart") (Deuteronomy 30:14).

It is the good news of salvation by faith which Paul and the other apostles preached.

10:9 Here it is in a nutshell. First you must accept the truth of the incarnation, that the Babe of Bethlehem's manger is the Lord of life and glory, that the Jesus of the New Testament is the Jehovah of the Old Testament.

Second, you must accept the truth of His resurrection, with all that it involves. God raised Him from the dead as proof that Christ had completed the work necessary for our salvation, and that God is satisfied with that work. Believing this with the heart means believing with one's mental, emotional, and volitional powers.

So you confess with your mouth Jesus as Lord and believe in your heart that God has raised Him from the dead. It is a personal appropriation of the Person and work of the Lord Jesus Christ. That is saving faith.

The question often arises, "Can a person be saved by accepting Jesus as Savior without also acknowledging Him as Lord?" The Bible gives no encouragement to anyone who believes with mental reservations: "I'll take Jesus as my Savior but I don't want to crown Him Lord of all." On the other hand, those who make submission to Jesus as Lord a condition of salvation face the problem, "To what degree must He be acknowledged as Lord?" Few Christians would claim to have made an absolute and complete surrender to Him in this way. When we present the gospel, we must maintain that faith is the sole condition of justification. And we must also remind sinners and saints constantly that Jesus Christ is Lord, and should be acknowledged as such.

10:10 In further explanation, Paul writes that man believes with the heart unto righteousness. It is not a mere intellectual assent but a genuine acceptance with one's whole inward being. When a man does that, he is instantly justified.

Then with the mouth confession is made unto salvation; that is, the believer publicly confesses the salvation he has already received. Confession is not a condition of salvation but the inevitable outward expression of what has happened. "If on Jesus Christ you trust, speak for Him you surely must." When a person really believes something, he wants to share it with others. So when a person is genuinely born again, it is too good to keep secret. He confesses Christ.

The Scriptures assume that when a person is saved he will make a public confession of that salvation. The two go together. Thus Kelly said, "If there be no confession of Christ the Lord with the mouth, we cannot speak of salvation; as our Lord said,

'He that believeth and is baptized shall be saved.' "[1] And Denney comments, "A heart believing unto righteousness, and a mouth making confession unto salvation, are not really two things, but two sides of the same thing."[2]

The question arises why confession comes first in 10:9, then belief, whereas in 10:10 belief comes first, then confession. The answer is not hard to find. In verse 9 the emphasis is on the incarnation and the resurrection, and these doctrines are mentioned in their chronological order. The incarnation comes first—Jesus is Lord. Then the resurrection—God raised Him from the dead. In verse 10 the emphasis is on the order of events in the salvation of a sinner. First he believes, then he makes a public confession of his salvation.

10:11 The apostle now quotes Isaiah 28:16 to emphasize that whoever believes on Him will not be put to shame. The thought of public confession of Christ might arouse fears of shame, but the opposite is true. Confession of Him on earth leads to His confession of us in heaven. Ours is a hope that will never be disappointed.

The word "whosoever" forms a link with what is to follow—namely, that God's glorious salvation is for all, Gentiles as well as Jews.

10:12 In Romans 3:23 we learned that there is no difference between Jew and Gentile as far as the need for salvation is concerned, for all are sinners. Now we learn that there is no difference as far as the availability of salvation is concerned. The Lord is not an exclusive God, but is Lord of all mankind. He pours out His grace and mercy abundantly to all those who call upon Him.

10:13 The words of Joel 2:32 are pressed into service to prove the universality of the gospel. One could scarcely wish for a simpler statement of the way of salvation than is found in these words: "Whosoever shall call upon the name of the Lord shall be saved." The name of the Lord stands for the Lord Himself.

10:14 But such a gospel presupposes a universal proclamation.

Of what use is a salvation offered to Jews and Gentiles if they never hear about it? Here we have the heartbeat of Christian missions!

In a series of four "how's" (how shall they call . . . believe . . . hear . . . preach), the apostle goes back over the steps that lead to the salvation of Jews and Gentiles. Perhaps it will be clearer if we reverse the order, as follows:

God sends His servants forth.

They preach the good news of salvation.

Sinners hear God's offer of life in Christ.

Some of those who hear believe the message.

Those who believe call on the Lord.

Those who call on Him are saved.

Hodge points out that this is an argument founded on the principle that if God wills the end, He also wills the means to reach that end.[3] This, as we have said, is the basis of the Christian missionary movement.

Paul is here vindicating his preaching the gospel to the Gentiles, a policy which the unbelieving Jews considered inexcusable.

10:15 God is the One who sends. We are the ones who are sent. What are we doing about it? Do we have the beautiful feet which Isaiah ascribed to those who bring glad tidings of good things (Isaiah 52:7)?

In the Isaiah passage we read of the beautiful feet of *Him*—that is, the Messiah. Here in Romans 10:15 the "him" becomes "them." *He* came with beautiful feet 1900 years ago. Now it is *our* privilege and responsibility to go with beautiful feet to a lost and dying world.

10:16 But the apostle's ever-present grief is that the people of Israel did not all listen to the gospel. Isaiah had prophesied as much when he asked, "Lord, who hath believed our report?" (Isaiah 53:1). The question calls for the answer, "Not many." When the announcement of the Messiah's first advent was heralded out, not many responded.

10:17 In this quotation from Isaiah, Paul notices that the belief spoken of by the prophet springs from the message that is heard, and that the message comes through the word about the Messiah. So he lays down the conclusion that "faith comes from what is heard, and what is heard comes by the preaching of [or about] Christ" (RSV). Faith comes to men when they hear our preaching concerning the Lord Jesus Christ, which is based, of course, on the written Word of God.

But hearing with the ears is not enough. A person must hear with an open heart and mind, willing to be shown the truth of God. If he does, he will find that the Word has the ring of truth, and that the truth is self-authenticating. He will then believe.

It should be clear, of course, that the "hearing" alluded to in this verse does not involve the ears exclusively. The message might be read, for example. So to hear means to receive the Word by whatever means.

10:18 What then has been the problem? Haven't both Jews and Gentiles heard the gospel preached? Yes. Paul borrows the words of Psalm 19:4 to show that they have. He says, "Yes verily, their sound went into all the earth, and their words unto the ends of the world." But the surprising thing is that these words from Psalm 19 are not speaking of the gospel at all. Rather, they describe the universal witness of the sun, moon, and stars to the glory of God. But as we said, Paul borrows them and says, in effect, that they are equally true of the worldwide proclamation of the gospel in his own day. By inspiration of the Spirit of God, the apostle often takes an Old Testament passage and applies it in quite a different way. The same Spirit who originally gave the words surely has the right to reapply them later on.

10:19 The call of the Gentiles and the rejection of the gospel by the majority of the Jews should not have come as a surprise to the nation of Israel. Their own Scriptures foretold exactly what would happen. For example, in Deuteronomy 32:21 God warned that He would provoke Israel to jealousy by a non-nation (the Gentiles), and anger Israel by a foolish, idolatrous people.

10:20 In even bolder language, Isaiah quotes the Lord as being found by the Gentiles, who weren't really looking for Him, and being revealed to those who weren't inquiring for Him (Isaiah 65:1).

Taken as a whole, the Gentiles didn't seek after God. They were satisfied with their pagan religions. But many of them did respond when they heard the gospel. Relatively speaking, the Gentiles responded more than the Jews did.

10:21 Against this picture of the Gentiles flocking to Jehovah, Isaiah portrays the Lord standing all day long with outstretched, beckoning hands to the nation of Israel, and being met with disobedience and stubborn refusal.

CHAPTER 11

11:1 What about the future of Israel? Is it true, as some teach, that God is through with Israel, that the church is now the Israel of God, and that all the promises to Israel now apply to the church? The eleventh chapter of Romans is one of the strongest refutations of that view in all the Bible.

Paul's opening question means, "Did God cast off his people *completely*? That is, has every single Israelite been cast off?" The point is that although God *has* cast off His people, as is distinctly stated in 11:15, this does not mean that He has rejected *all* of them. Paul himself is a proof that the casting away has not been complete. After all, he was an Israelite, of the seed of Abraham, and of the tribe of Benjamin. His credentials as a Jew were impeccable.

11:2 So we must understand the first part of this verse as saying, "God has not *completely* cast off his people which he foreknew." The situation was similar to that which existed in the time of Elijah. The mass of the nation had turned away from God to idols. Conditions were so bad that Elijah prayed against his people instead of for them.

11:3 He complained to God that the people had silenced the voice of the prophets in death. They had destroyed the altars of the Lord. It seemed to him that his was the only faithful voice for God that was left, and his life was in imminent danger.

11:4 But the picture wasn't as dark and hopeless as Elijah feared. God reminded the prophet that He had preserved for Himself 7000 men who had steadfastly refused to follow the nation in Baal-worship.

11:5 What was true then is true now: God never leaves Himself without a witness. He always has a faithful remnant chosen by Himself as special objects of His grace.

11:6 God doesn't choose this remnant on the basis of their works, but by His sovereign, electing grace. These two principles—grace and works—are mutually exclusive. A gift cannot be earned. What is free cannot be bought. What is unmerited cannot be deserved. Fortunately, God's choice was based on grace, not on works; otherwise no one could ever have been chosen.

11:7 The conclusion, then, is that the nation failed to obtain righteousness because they sought it through self-effort instead of through the finished work of Christ. The remnant, chosen by God, succeeded in obtaining righteousness through faith in the Lord Jesus. The nation suffered what might be called a judicial hardening. Refusal to receive the Messiah resulted in a decreased capacity and inclination to receive Him.

11:8 This is exactly what the Old Testament predicted would happen (Isaiah 29:10; Deuteronomy 29:4). God abandoned them to a state of stupor in which they became insensitive to spiritual realities. Because they refused to see the Lord Jesus as Messiah and Savior, now they lost the power to see Him. Because they would not hear the pleading voice of God, now they were smitten with spiritual deafness. That terrible judgment continues to the present day.

11:9 David, too, anticipated the judgment of God on Israel. In Psalm 69:22,23 he described the rejected Savior as calling on God to turn their table into a snare and a trap. The table here means the sum total of the privileges and blessings which flowed through Christ. What should have been a blessing was turned into a curse.

11:10 In the Psalms passage, the suffering Savior also called on God to let their eyes be blinded and their bodies bent over as by toil or in old age (or, their loins made to shake continually).

11:17 The apostle continues the metaphor of the root and the branches.

". . . if some of the branches be broken off." These branches refer to the unbelieving portion of the 12 tribes of Israel. Because of their rejection of the Messiah, they were removed from their place of privilege as God's chosen people. But only some of the branches were removed. A remnant of the nation, including Paul himself, had received the Lord.

"and thou, being a wild olive tree, were grafted in among them." The wild olive tree refers to the Gentiles, viewed as one people. They were grafted in to the olive tree.

"and with them partakest of the root and fatness of the olive tree." The Gentiles share the position of favor that had originally been given to Israel and is still held by the believing remnant of Israel.

In this illustration it is important to see that the main trunk of the olive tree is not Israel, but rather God's line of privilege down through the centuries. If the trunk is Israel, then you have the bizarre picture of Israel being broken off from Israel and then grafted back into Israel again.

It is also important to remember that the wild olive branch is not the church but the Gentiles viewed collectively. Otherwise you face the possibility of true believers being cut off from God's favor. Paul has already shown that this is impossible (Romans 8:38,39).

When we say that the trunk of the tree is the line of privilege down through the centuries, what do we mean by "line of privilege"? God decided to set apart a certain people to occupy a special place of nearness to Himself. They would be set apart from the rest of the world and would have special privileges. They would enjoy what we today might call the "favored-nation status." In the different ages of history, He would have a special inner circle.

The nation of Israel was the first to be in this line of privilege. They were God's ancient, chosen, earthly people. Because of their rejection of the Messiah, some of these branches were broken off and thus lost their position of "favorite son." The Gentiles were grafted into the olive tree and became partakers with believing Jews of the root and of the fatness. The root points back to Abraham, with whom the line of privilege began. The fatness of an olive tree refers to its productivity—that is, to its rich crop of olives and the oil derived from them. Here the fatness signifies the privileges that flowed from union with the olive tree.

11:18 But the Gentiles should not take a holier-than-thou attitude toward the Jews, or boast of any superiority. Any such boasting overlooks the fact that they didn't originate the line of privilege. Rather, it is the line of privilege that put them where they are, in a place of special favor.

11:19 Paul anticipates that the imaginary Gentile with whom he has been conversing will say, "The Jewish branches were broken off so that I and other Gentile branches might be grafted in."

11:20 The apostle admits that the statement is partially true. The word "Well" in the KJV indicates approval. The NASB translates "Quite right!" The Jewish branches *were* broken off, and the Gentiles were grafted in. But it was because of the unbelief of Israel and not because the Gentiles had any special claim on God. The Gentiles were grafted in because, as a people, they stood by faith. This expression, "thou standest by faith," seems to indicate that Paul is speaking about true believers. But that is not necessarily the meaning. The only way in which the Gentiles stood by faith was that, comparatively speaking, they demonstrated more faith than the Jews did. Thus Jesus said to a Gentile centurion, "I have not found so great faith, no, not in Israel" (Luke 7:9). And Paul later said to the Jews at Rome, "Be it known therefore unto you that the salvation of God is sent unto the Gentiles, and that they will hear it" (Acts 28:28). Notice, "they will hear it." This is how the Gentiles can be said to stand by faith. As a people they are more receptive to the gospel today than Israel. To *stand* here is the opposite of to *fall*. Israel had fallen from its place of privilege. The Gentiles had been grafted into that place.

But let him who stands beware lest he falls. Gentiles should not be puffed up with pride but should maintain an attitude of reverential fear.

11:21 If God didn't hesitate to cut off the natural branches from the line of privilege, there is no reason to believe that he would spare the wild olive branches under similar circumstances.

11:22 So in the parable of the olive tree, we see two great contrasting facets of God's character—His goodness and His severity. His severity is manifest in the removal of Israel from the favored-nation status. His goodness is seen in His turning to the Gentiles with the gospel (see Acts 13:46; 18:6). But that goodness must not be taken for granted. The Gentiles too could be cut off if they do not maintain that relative openness which the Savior found during His earthly ministry (Matthew 8:10; Luke 7:9).

It must be constantly borne in mind that Paul is not speaking of the church or of individual believers. He is speaking about the Gentiles as such. Nothing can ever separate the Body of Christ from the Head, and nothing can separate a believer from the love of God, but the Gentile peoples can be removed from their present position of special privilege.

11:23 And Israel's severance need not be final. If they abandon their national unbelief, there is no reason why God cannot put them back into their original place of privilege. It would not be impossible for God to do this.

11:24 In fact, it would be a much less violent process for God to reinstate Israel as His privileged people than it was to put the Gentiles into that place. The people of Israel were the original branches in the tree of God's favor, and so they are called the natural branches. The Gentile branches came from a wild olive tree. To graft a wild olive branch into a good olive tree is an unnatural graft, or, as Paul says, it is contrary to nature. To graft natural branches into their original good olive tree is a very natural process.

11:25 Now the apostle reveals that the future restoration of Israel is not only a possibility but is an assured fact. What Paul now reveals is a mystery—a truth hitherto unknown, a truth that could not be known by man's unaided intellect, but a truth that has now been made known. Paul sets it forth so that Gentile believers will not be wise in their own conceits, looking down their nationalistic noses at the Jews. The mystery is as follows.

A hardening in part has befallen Israel. It has not affected all the nation, but only the unbelieving segment.

That hardening is temporary. It will continue only until the fullness of the Gentiles arrives. The fullness of the Gentiles refers to the time when the last member will be added to the church, and when the completed Body of Christ will be raptured home to heaven. The fullness of the Gentiles must be distinguished from the times of the Gentiles (Luke 21:24). The fullness of the Gentiles coincides with the Rapture. The times of the Gentiles refer to the entire period of Gentile domination over the Jews, beginning with the Babylonian captivity (2 Chronicles 36:1-21) and ending with Christ's return to earth to reign.

11:26 While Israel's judicial hardness is removed at the time of the Rapture, that does not mean that all Israel will be saved right away. Jews will be converted throughout the Tribulation period, but the entire elect remnant will not be saved until Christ returns to earth as King of kings and Lord of lords.

When Paul says that all Israel shall be saved, we must understand that he means all *believing* Israel. The unbelieving portion of the nation will be destroyed at the second advent of Christ (Zechariah 13:8,9). Only those who say "Blessed is He who comes in the name of the Lord" will be spared to enter the kingdom.

This is what Isaiah referred to when he spoke of the Deliverer coming to Zion and turning ungodliness away from Jacob (Isaiah 59:20). Notice that it is not Christ's coming to Bethlehem, but His coming to Zion—that is, His second coming.

11:27 It is the same time referred to in Isaiah 27:9 and Jeremiah 31:33,34, when God shall take away their sins under the terms of the New Covenant.

11:28 So we might summarize Israel's present status by saying first that "As concerning the gospel, they are enemies for your sakes." They are enemies in the sense of being cast off, set aside, alienated from God's favor so that the gospel might go forth to the Gentiles.

But that is only half the picture. As far as the election is concerned, they are beloved for the father's sake—that is, for the sake of Abraham, Isaac, and Jacob.

11:29 The reason they are still beloved is that God's gifts and callings are never rescinded. God does not take back His gifts. Once He has made an unconditional promise, He never goes back on it. He gave Israel the special privileges listed in 9:4,5. He called Israel to be His earthly people (Isaiah 48:12), separate from the rest of the nations. Nothing can change His purposes.

11:30 The Gentiles were originally an untamed, disobedient people, but when Israel spurned the Messiah and the gospel of salvation, God turned to the Gentiles in mercy.

11:31 A somewhat similar sequence of events will occur in the future. Israel's disobedience will be followed by mercy, when they are provoked to jealousy through the mercy shown to the Gentiles. Some teach that it is through the Gentiles' showing mercy to the Jews that they will be restored, but we know that this is not so. Israel's restoration will be brought about by the second advent of the Lord Jesus (see 11:26,27).

11:32 When we first read this verse, we might get the idea that God arbitrarily condemned both Jews and Gentiles to unbelief, and that there was nothing they could do about it. But that, of course, is not the thought at all. The unbelief was their own doing. What the verse is saying is this: having found both Jews and Gentiles to be disobedient, God is pictured as imprisoning them both in that condition, so that there would be no way out for them except on His terms.

This disobedience provided scope for God to show mercy to all, both Jews and Gentiles. There is no suggestion here of universal salvation. God has shown mercy to the Gentiles and will yet show mercy to the Jews also, but this does not insure the salvation of everyone. Here it is mercy shown along national lines.

"God having tested both the Hebrew and the Gentile nations, and both having broken down under the test, He shut them up in unbelief so that, being manifestly without merit, and having by demonstration forfeited all claims and all rights to divine favor, He might, in the unsearchable riches of His grace, have mercy upon them all."[1]

11:33 This concluding doxology looks back over the entire letter and the divine wonders that have been unfolded. Paul has expounded the marvelous plan of salvation by which a just God can save ungodly sinners and still be just in doing so. He has shown how Christ's work brought more glory to God and more blessing to men than Adam lost through his sin. He has explained how grace produces holy living in a way that law could never do. He has traced the unbreakable chain of God's purpose from foreknowledge to eventual glorification. He has set forth the doctrine of sovereign election and the companion doctrine of human responsibility. And he has traced the justice and harmony of God's dispensational dealings with Israel and the nations. Now nothing could be more appropriate than to burst forth in a hymn of praise and worship.

"O the depth of the riches, the wisdom and the knowledge of God" (NIV)!

The riches of God! He is rich in mercy, love, grace, faithfulness, power, and goodness.

The wisdom of God! His wisdom is infinite, unsearchable, incomparable, and invincible.

The knowledge of God! "God is omniscient. He knows everything: everything possible, everything actual; all events, all creatures, of the past, the present, and the future."[2]

His decisions are unsearchable; they are too deep for mortal minds to fully understand. The ways in which He arranges creation, history, redemption, and providence are beyond our limited comprehension.

11:34 No created being can know the mind of God except to the extent that He chooses to reveal it. And even then we see through a glass darkly (1 Corinthians 13:12).

No one is qualified to advise God. He doesn't need our counsel, and wouldn't profit by it anyway (see Isaiah 40:13).

11:35 No one has ever made God obligated to him (see Job 41:11). What gift of ours would ever put the Eternal in a position where He had to repay?

11:36 The Almighty is self-contained. He is the source of every good, He is the active Agent in sustaining and controlling the universe, and He is the Object for which everything has been created. Everything is designed to bring glory to Him.

Let it be so! "To Him be the glory forever. Amen."

CHAPTER 12

The rest of the epistle answers the question: *How should those who have been justified by grace respond in their everyday lives?* Paul takes up our duties toward other believers, toward the community, toward our enemies, toward the government, and toward our weaker brothers.

12:1 Serious and devout consideration of the mercies of God, as they have been set forth in chapters 1 through 11, leads to only one conclusion—we should present our bodies as living sacrifices, holy and acceptable to God. Our bodies stand for all our members and also (by extension) for our entire lives.

Total commitment is both our reasonable service (KJV) and our spiritual worship (NIV). It is our reasonable service in this sense: if the Son of God has died for me, then the least I can do is live for Him. "If Jesus Christ is God and died for me, then no sacrifice can be too great for me to make for him."[1] "Love so amazing, so divine, demands my heart, my life, my all."[2]

Total commitment is also our spiritual worship. As believer-priests, we do not come to God with the bodies of slain animals but with the spiritual sacrifice of yielded lives. We also offer to Him our service (Romans 15:16), our praise (Hebrews 13:15), and our possessions (Hebrews 13:16).

12:2 Secondly, Paul urges us not to be conformed to the world, or as Phillips' paraphrase renders it: "Don't let the world around you squeeze you into its own mold." When we come to the kingdom of God, we should abandon the thought-patterns and lifestyles of the world.

The *world* or *age* as used here means the society or system that man has built in order to make himself happy without God. It is a kingdom that is antagonistic to God.

The god and prince of this world is Satan (2 Corinthians 4:4; John 12:31; 14:30; 16:11). All unconverted people are his subjects. He seeks to attract and hold people through the lust of the eyes, the lust of the flesh, and the pride of life (1 John 2:16).

The world has its own politics, art, music, religion, amusements, thought-patterns, and lifestyles, and it seeks to get everyone to conform to its culture and customs. It hates nonconformists—like Christ and His followers.

Christ died to deliver us from this world. The world is crucified to us, and we are crucified to the world. It would be absolute disloyalty to the Lord for believers to love the world. Anyone who loves the world is an enemy of God.

Believers are not of the world any more than Christ is of the world. However, they are sent into the world to testify that its works are evil and that salvation is available to all who put their faith in the Lord Jesus Christ.

We should not only be separated from the world; we should be *transformed* by the renewing of our minds, which means that we should think the way God thinks, as revealed in the Bible.

Then we can experience the direct guidance of God in our lives. And we will find that, instead of being distasteful and hard, His will is good and acceptable and perfect.

Here, then, are three keys for knowing God's will. The first is a yielded body, the second a separated life, and the third a transformed mind.

12:3 Paul speaks here through the grace that was given to him as an apostle of the Lord Jesus. He is going to deal with various forms of straight and crooked thinking.

First he says that there is nothing in the gospel that would encourage anyone to have a superiority complex. He urges us to be humble in exercising our gifts. We should not have exaggerated ideas of our own importance. Neither should we be envious of others. Rather, we should realize that each person is unique and that we all have an important function to perform for our Lord.

We should be happy with the place God has given us in the Body, and we should seek to exercise our gifts with all the strength that God supplies.

12:4 The human body has many members, yet each one has a unique role to play. The health and welfare of the body depend on the proper functioning of each member.

12:5 That is how it is in the Body of Christ. There is unity (one Body), diversity (we . . . are many), and interdependency (members of one another). Any gifts we have are not for selfish use or display but for the good of the Body. No gift is self-sufficient and none is unnecessary. When we realize all this, we are thinking soberly (12:3).

12:6 Paul now gives instructions for the use of certain gifts. The list does not cover all the gifts; it is meant to be suggestive rather than exhaustive.

Our gifts differ according to the grace that is given to us. In other words, God's grace deals out differing gifts to different people. And God gives the necessary strength or ability to use whatever gifts we have. So we are responsible to use these God-given abilities as good stewards.

Those who have the gift of prophecy should prophesy according to the proportion of faith. A prophet is a spokesman for God, declaring the Word of the Lord. Prediction may be involved, but it is not a necessary element of prophecy. In the early church the prophets were "men who spoke under the immediate influence of the Spirit of God, and delivered some divine communication relative to doctrinal truths, to present duty, to future events, as the case may be."[3] Their ministry is preserved for us in the pages of the New Testament. There can be no inspired, prophetic additions to the body of Christian doctrine today since the faith has been once-for-all delivered unto the saints (see Jude 3 NASB). Thus a prophet today is simply one who declares the mind of God as it has been revealed in the Bible. "All modern prophecy that is true is but the republication of Christ's message—the proclamation and expounding of truth already revealed in Scripture."[4]

Paul says that any of us who has the gift of prophecy should prophesy according to the proportion of faith. This may mean "according to the rule or norm of the faith"—that is, in accordance with the doctrines of the Christian faith as they are found in the Scriptures. Or it may mean "according to the proportion of our faith"—that is, to the extent that God gives us faith. Most modern versions supply the word "our" here, but it is not found in the original.

12:7 Ministry is a very broad term meaning service for the Lord. It does not mean the office, duties, or functions of a clergyman (as the word is commonly used today). The person who has the gift of ministry has a servant-heart. He sees opportunities to be of service and seizes them.

The teacher is one who is able to explain the Word of God and apply it to the hearts of his hearers.

Whatever our gift is, we should give ourselves to it whole-heartedly.

12:8 Exhortation is the gift of stirring up the saints to desist from every form of evil and to press on to new achievements for Christ in holiness and in service.

Giving is the divine endowment which inclines and empowers a person to be aware of needs and to help meet them. He should do so with liberality.

The gift of ruling is almost certainly connected with the work of elders (and perhaps also deacons) in a local church. The elder is an undershepherd who stands out in front of the flock and leads with care and diligence.

The gift of mercy is the supernatural capacity and talent of aiding those who are in distress. Those who have this gift should exercise it with cheerfulness. Of course, we should all show mercy and do it cheerfully.

A Christian lady once said to me, "When my mother became old and needed someone to care for her, my husband and I invited her to come and live with us. I did all I could to make her comfortable. I cooked for her, did her washing, took her out in the car, and generally cared for all her needs. But while I was going through the motions outwardly, I was unhappy inside. Subconsciously I resented the interruption of our usual schedule. Sometimes my mother would say to me, 'You never smile anymore. Why don't you ever smile?' You see, I was showing mercy, but I wasn't doing it with cheerfulness.''

12:9 In 12:9-19 the apostle lists some characteristics that every believer should develop in his dealings with other Christians and with the unconverted.

Love should be without hypocrisy. It should not wear a mask, but should be genuine, sincere, and unaffected.

We should abhor all forms of evil and hold onto everything that is good. In this setting ''evil'' probably means all attitudes and acts of unlove, malice, and hatred. ''Good,'' by contrast, means every manifestation of supernatural love.

12:10 In our relations with those who are in the household of faith, we should demonstrate our love by tender affection, not by cool indifference or routine acceptance.

We should prefer to see others honored rather than ourselves. I remember reading of a beloved servant of Christ who was in a sideroom with other notables before a meeting. Several had already moved onto the platform before it was his turn. When he appeared at the door, thunderous applause broke out for him. He quickly stepped aside and applauded so that he would not share the honor that he sincerely thought was intended for the others.

12:11 Moffatt's helpful translation of this verse is: ''Never let your zeal flag, maintain the spiritual glow, serve the Lord.'' Here we are reminded of the words of Jeremiah 48:10: ''Cursed be he that doeth the work of Jehovah negligently'' (ASV).

> 'Tis not for man to trifle; life is brief
>   And sin is here.
> Our age is but the falling of a leaf,
>   A dropping tear.
> We have no time to sport away the hours;
>   All must be earnest in a world like ours.
>   —Horatius Bonar

12:12 No matter what our present circumstances may be, we can and should rejoice in our hope—the coming of our Savior, the redemption of our bodies, and our eternal glory.

We are exhorted to be patient in tribulation—that is, to bear up bravely under it. As someone has said, "This all-conquering endurance is the one thing which can turn affliction into glory."

We should continue steadfastly in prayer. It is in prayer that the work is done and victories are won. Prayer brings power in our lives and peace to our hearts. When we pray in the Name of the Lord Jesus, we come the closest to omnipotence that it is possible for mortal man to come. Therefore we do ourselves a great disservice when we neglect our prayer life.

12:13 Needy saints are everywhere—the unemployed, those who have been drained by medical bills, forgotten preachers and missionaries in obscure places, and senior citizens whose resources have dwindled. True body-life means sharing with those who are in need.

"Never grudging a meal or a bed to those who need them" (Phillips). Hospitality is a lost art. Small homes and apartments are used as excuses for not receiving Christians who are passing through. Perhaps we do not want to face the added work and inconvenience. But we forget that when we entertain God's children, it is the same as if we were entertaining the Lord Himself. Our homes should be like the home in Bethany, where Jesus loved to be.

12:14 We are called to show kindness toward our persecutors instead of trying to repay them in kind. It requires divine life to repay unkindness and injury with a courtesy. The natural response is to curse and retaliate.

12:15 Empathy is the capacity for sharing vicariously the feelings and emotions of others. Our tendency is to be jealous when others rejoice, and to pass by when they mourn. God's way is to enter into the joys and sorrows of those around us.

12:16 To be of the same mind toward one another does not mean that we must see alike on nonessential matters. It is not so much uniformity of mind as harmony of relationships.

We should avoid any trace of snobbishness and should be as outgoing toward humble, lowly folk as toward those of wealth and position. When an illustrious Christian arrived at the terminal he was met by leaders from the assembly where he was to speak. The limousine pulled up to take him to a plush hotel. "Who usually entertains the preachers here?" he asked. They mentioned an elderly couple in a modest home nearby. "That's where I would prefer to stay," he said.

Again, the apostle warns against a believer being wise in his own conceits. The realization that we have nothing that we did not receive should keep us from an inflated ego.

12:17 Repaying evil with evil is common practice in the world. Men speak of giving tit for tat, of repaying in kind, or of giving someone what he deserves. But this delight in vengeance should have no place in the lives of those who have been redeemed. Instead, they should act honorably in the face of abuse and injury, as in all the circumstances of life. To *provide* in this verse means to *take thought for* or *be careful to do*.

12:18 Christians should not be needlessly provocative or contentious. The righteousness of God is not worked out by belligerence and wrath. We should love peace, make peace, and be at peace. When we have offended others, or when someone has offended us, we should work tirelessly for a peaceful resolution of the matter.

12:19 We must resist the tendency to avenge wrongs that are done against us. The expression "give place unto wrath" may mean to allow God to take care of it for you, or it may mean to submit passively in a spirit of nonresistance. The rest of the verse favors the first interpretation—to stand back and let the wrath of God take care of it. Vengeance is God's prerogative. We should not interfere with what is His right. He will repay at the proper time and in the proper manner. "God has long ago settled the whole matter about exacting justice from wrongdoers. Not one of them will escape. Perfect justice will be done in every case and will be done perfectly. If any of us interfered, it would be the height of presumption."[5]

12:20 Christianity goes beyond nonresistance to active benevolence. It does not destroy its enemies by violence but converts them by love. It feeds the enemy when he is hungry and satisfies his thirst, thus heaping live coals on his head. If the live coal treatment seems cruel, it is because it is not properly understood. To heap live coals on a person's head means to make him ashamed of his hostility by surprising him with unconventional kindness.

12:21 Darby explains the first part of this verse as follows: "If my bad temper puts you in a bad temper, you have been overcome of evil."[6]

George Washington Carver once said, "I will never let another man ruin my life by making me hate him."[7] He would not allow evil to conquer him.

"But overcome evil with good." It is characteristic of Christian teaching that it does not stop with the negative prohibition but goes on to the positive exhortation. Evil can be overpowered with good. This is a weapon we should use more frequently.

Stanton treated Lincoln with venomous hatred. He said that it was foolish to go to Africa in search of a gorilla when the original gorilla could be found in Springfield, Illinois. Lincoln took it all in stride.

Later Lincoln appointed Stanton as war minister, feeling that he was the most qualified for the office.

After Lincoln was shot, Stanton called him the greatest leader of men. Love had conquered!

CHAPTER 13

13:1 Those who have been justified by faith are obligated to be subject to human government. Actually the obligation applies to everyone, but the apostle here is concerned especially with believers.

God established human government after the flood when He decreed, "Whoso sheddeth man's blood, by man shall his blood be shed" (Genesis 9:6). That decree gave authority to men to judge criminal matters and to punish offenders.

In every ordered society there must be authority and submission to that authority. Otherwise you have a state of anarchy, and you cannot survive indefinitely under anarchy. Any government is better than no government.

So God has instituted human government, and no government exists apart from His will. This does not mean that He approves of all that human rulers do. He certainly does not approve of corruption, brutality, and tyranny. But the fact remains that "there is no government anywhere that God has not placed in power" (TLB).

Believers can live victoriously in a democracy, a constitutional monarchy, or even a totalitarian regime. No earthly government is any better than the men who comprise it. That is why none of our governments is perfect. The only ideal government is a beneficent monarchy with the Lord Jesus Christ as King.

It is helpful to remember that Paul wrote this section on subjection to human government when the infamous Nero was Emperor of Rome. Those were dark days for the Christians. Nero blamed them for a fire which destroyed half the city (and which he himself may have ordered). He caused some believers to be immersed in tar, then ignited as living torches to provide illumination for his garden parties. Others were sewn up in animal skins, then thrown to ferocious dogs to be torn to pieces.

13:2 And yet it still holds that anyone who disobeys or rebels against the government is disobeying and rebelling against what God has ordained. Those who resist lawful authority earn and deserve punishment.

There is an exception, of course. A Christian is not required to obey if the government orders him to sin or to compromise his loyalty to Jesus Christ (Acts 5:29). No government has a right to command a person's conscience. So there are times when a believer must, by obeying God, incur the wrath of man. In such cases he must be prepared to pay the penalty without undue complaint. Under no circumstances should he rebel against the government or join in an attempt to overthrow it.

13:3 As a general rule, people who do what is right need not fear the authorities. It is only those who break the law who have to fear punishment. So if anyone wants to enjoy a life free from tickets, fines, trials, and imprisonments, the thing to do is to be a law-abiding citizen. Then he will win the approval of the authorities, not their censure.

13:4 The ruler, whether he is a president, governor, mayor, or judge, is a minister of God in the sense that he is a servant and representative of the Lord. He may not know God personally, but he is still the Lord's man officially. Thus David repeatedly referred to the wicked King Saul as the Lord's anointed (1 Samuel 24:6,10; 26:9,11,16,23). In spite of Saul's repeated attempts on David's life, the latter would not allow his men to harm the king. Why? Because Saul was the king, and as such he was the Lord's appointee.

As servants of God, rulers are expected to promote the good of the people—their security, tranquility, and general welfare. If any man insists on breaking the law, he can expect to pay for it, because the government has the authority to bring him to trial and punish him.

In the expression "he beareth not the sword in vain" we have a strong statement concerning the power which God vests in the government. The sword is not just an innocuous symbol of power; a scepter would have served that purpose. The sword seems to speak of the ultimate power of the ruler—that is, to inflict capital punishment. So it will not do to say that capital punishment was for the Old Testament era only and not for the New. Here is a statement in the New Testament that implies that the government has the authority to take the life of a capital offender. People argue against this by quoting Exodus 20:13: "Thou shalt not kill." But that commandment refers to murder, and capital punishment is not murder. Capital punishment was prescribed in the Old Testament law as the required punishment for certain serious offenses.

Again the apostle reminds us that the ruler is "a minister of God," but this time he adds, "an avenger for wrath to him that doeth evil" (ASV). In other words, in addition to being a minister of God to us for good, he also serves God by dispensing punishment to those who break the law.

13:5 What this means is that we should be obedient subjects of the government for two reasons—the fear of punishment and the desire to maintain a good conscience.

13:6 We owe the government not only obedience but financial support through the payment of taxes. It is to our advantage to live in a society of law and order, with police and fire protection, so we must be willing to bear our share of the cost involved. Government officials are giving their time and talents in carrying out God's will for the maintenance of a stable society, so they are entitled to support.

13:7 The fact that believers are citizens of heaven (Philippians 3:20 NEB) does not exempt them from responsibility to human government. They must pay whatever taxes are levied on their income, their real estate, and their personal property. They must pay required custom on merchandise being transported from one country to another. They must demonstrate a respectful fear of displeasing those who are charged with enforcing the laws. And they must show respect for the names and offices of all civil servants (even if they can't always respect their personal lives).

In this connection, Christians should never join in speaking in a derogatory way of the President of the country. Even in the heat of a political campaign they should refuse to join in the verbal abuse that is heaped upon the head of state. It is written, "Thou shalt not speak evil of the ruler of thy people" (Acts 23:5).

13:8 Basically, the first part of this verse means "Pay your bills on time." It is not a prohibition against any form of debt. Some kinds of debt are inevitable in our society: most of us face monthly bills for telephone, gas, light, water, etc. And it is impossible to manage a business without contracting some debts. The admonition here is not to get into arrears (overdue accounts).

But in addition there are certain principles which should guide us in this area. We should not contract debts for nonessentials. We should not go into debt when there is no hope of repaying. We should avoid buying on the installment plan, incurring exorbitant interest charges. We should avoid borrowing to buy a product that depreciates in value. In general, we should practice financial responsibility by living modestly and within our means, always remembering that the borrower is slave to the lender (see Proverbs 22:7).

The one debt that is always outstanding is the obligation to love. The word that is used for *love* in Romans, with only one exception (12:10), is *agape,* which signifies a deep, unselfish, superhuman affection which one person has for another. This otherworldly love is not activated by any virtue in the person loved; that is, it is completely undeserved. It is unlike any other love in that it goes out not only to the lovable but to one's enemies as well.

This love manifests itself in giving, and generally in sacrificial giving. Thus, God so loved the world that He gave His only-begotten Son. Christ loved the church and gave Himself for it.

It is primarily a matter of the will rather than the emotions.

The fact that we are commanded to love indicates that it is something we can choose to do. If it were an uncontrollable emotion that swept over us at unexpected moments, we could scarcely be held accountable. This does not deny, however, that the emotions can be involved.

It is impossible for an unconverted person to manifest this divine love. In fact, it is impossible even for a believer to demonstrate it in his own strength. It can only be exhibited by the power of the indwelling Holy Spirit.

Love found its perfect expression on earth in the Person of the Lord Jesus Christ.

Our love to God manifests itself in obedience to His commandments.

The man who loves his neighbor has fulfilled the law, or at least that section of the law which teaches love for our fellowmen.

13:9 The apostle singles out those commandments which forbid acts of unlove against one's neighbor. They are the commandments against adultery, murder, theft, perjury, and coveting. Love doesn't exploit another person's body; immorality does. Love doesn't take another person's life; murder does. Love doesn't steal another person's property; theft does. Love doesn't deny justice to others; false witness does. Love doesn't even entertain wrong desires for another person's possessions; coveting does. (Actually, the clause "Thou shalt not bear false witness" is omitted in the best manuscripts, but it is a social duty comprehended in the obligation to love one's neighbor.)

"And if there be any other commandment." Paul could have mentioned one other: "Honor thy father and thy mother." They all boil down to the same dictum: "Love your neighbor as yourself." Treat him with the same affection, consideration, and kindness that you treat yourself.

13:10 Love never seeks to harm another. Rather, it actively seeks the welfare and honor of all. Therefore the man who acts in love is really filling the requirements of the second table of the law.

13:11 The rest of the chapter encourages a life of spiritual alertness and moral purity. The time is short. The dispensation of grace is drawing to a close. The lateness of the hour demands that all lethargy and inactivity be put away. Our salvation is nearer than ever. The Savior is coming to take us to the Father's house.

13:12 This present age is like a night of sin that has just about run its course. The day of eternal glory is about to dawn for believers. This means that we should throw off all the filthy garments of worldliness—that is, everything that is associated with unrighteousness and evil. And we should put on the armor of light, which means the protective covering of a holy life. The pieces of armor are detailed in Ephesians 6:14-18. They describe the elements of true Christian character.

13:13 Notice that the emphasis is on our practical Christian walk. Since we are children of the day, we should walk as sons of light. What does a Christian have to do with wild parties, with drunken brawls, with sex orgies, with vile excesses, or even with bickering and envy? Nothing at all.

13:14 The best policy we can follow is, first of all, to put on the Lord Jesus Christ. This means that we should adopt His whole lifestyle, live as He lived, accept Him as our Guide and Example.

Secondly, we should not make provision for the flesh, to fulfill its lusts. The flesh here is the old, corrupt nature. It incessantly cries to be pampered with comfort, luxury, illicit sexual indulgence, empty amusements, worldly pleasures, dissipation, materialism, etc. We make provision for the flesh when we buy things that are associated with temptation, when we make it easy for ourselves to sin, when we give a higher priority to the physical than to the spiritual. We should not indulge the flesh even a little. Rather, as Phillips says, we should ''give no chances to the flesh to have its fling.''

CHAPTER 14

14:1 The passage from 14:1 to 15:13 deals with important principles to guide God's people in dealing with matters of secondary importance. These are the matters that so often cause conflict among believers, but such conflict is quite unnecessary, as we shall see.

The weak brother is one who has unfounded scruples over matters of secondary importance. In this context, he was probably a converted Jew who still had scruples about eating nonkosher foods or working on Saturday.

The first principle is this: the weak brother should be received into the local fellowship, but not with the idea of engaging him in disputes about his ultrascrupulousness. Christians can have happy fellowship without agreeing on nonessentials.

14:2 A believer who walks in the full enjoyment of his Christian liberty has faith, based on the teachings of the New Testament, that all foods are clean (Mark 7:19 NASB). They are sanctified by the Word of God and prayer (1 Timothy 4:4,5).

A believer with a weak conscience may have qualms about eating pork, or any other meat, for that matter. He may be a vegetarian.

14:3 So the second principle is that there must be mutual forbearance. The mature Christian must not put down his weak brother. Neither should the weak brother condemn as a sinner the one who enjoys ham, shrimp, or lobster. God has received him into His family, a member in good standing.

14:4 The third principle is that each believer is a servant of the Lord, and we have no right to sit in judgment, as if we were the master. It is before his own Master that each one stands approved or disapproved.

One may look down on the other with icy condescension, sure that he will make shipwreck of the faith because of his views on these matters. But such an attitude is wrong. God will sustain those on both sides of the question. His power to do so is adequate.

14:5 Some of the early Jewish Christians still looked on the Sabbath as a day of obligation. They had a conscience about doing any work on Saturday. In that sense, they esteemed one day above another.

The other believers did not share these Judaistic scruples. They looked on every day alike. They did not look upon six days as secular and one as sacred. To them all days were sacred.

But what about the Lord's Day, the first day of the week? Does it not have a special place in the lives of Christians? We see in the New Testament that it was the day of our Lord's resurrection (Luke 24:1-9). On the next two Lord's Days, Christ met with His disciples (John 20:19,26). The Holy Spirit was given on the Day of Pentecost, which was on the first day of the week; Pentecost occurred seven Sundays after the Feast of Firstfruits (Leviticus 23:15,16; Acts 2:1), which symbolizes Christ's resurrection (1 Corinthians 15:20,23). The disciples gathered to break bread on the first day of the week (Acts 20:7). Paul instructed the Corinthians to take a collection on the first day of the week. So the Lord's Day does stand out in the New Testament in a special way. But rather than being a day of obligation, like the Sabbath, it is a day of privilege. Released from our ordinary employment, we can set it apart in a special way for worshiping and serving our Lord.

Nowhere in the New Testament are Christians ever told to keep the Sabbath. And yet at the same time we recognize the principle of one day in seven, one day of rest after six days of work.

Whatever view one holds on this subject, the principle is this: let everyone be fully persuaded in his own mind. Now it should be clear that such a principle applies only to matters that are morally neutral. When it comes to the fundamental doctrines of the Christian faith, there is no room for individual opinions. But in this area where things are neither right nor wrong in themselves, there is room for differing views. They should not be allowed to become tests of fellowship.

14:6 The one who regards the day, in this verse, is a Jewish believer who still has a bad conscience about doing any work on Saturday. It is not that he looks upon Sabbath-keeping as a means of obtaining or retaining salvation; it is simply a matter of doing what he thinks will please the Lord.

Most modern versions omit the clause "and he that regardeth not the day, to the Lord he doth not regard it." In his *Expository Dictionary,* Vine says, "The Scripture does not speak of not regarding a day."

The man who has liberty to eat nonkosher foods bows his head and gives thanks for them. So does the believer with the weak conscience, who eats only kosher foods. Both men ask the blessing from God.

In both cases God is honored and thanked, so why should this be made the occasion of strife and conflict?

14:7 The Lordship of Christ enters into every aspect of the life of a believer. We don't live to ourselves but to the Lord. We don't die to ourselves but to the Lord.

It is true that what we do and say affects others, but that is not the thought in this verse. Here Paul is emphasizing that the Lord should be the goal and object of the lives of His people.

14:8 Everything we do in life is subject to Christ's scrutiny and approval. We test things by how they appear in His presence.

Even in death we aspire to glorify the Lord as we go to be with Him.

Both in life and in death we belong to Him.

14:9 One of the reasons for which Christ died and rose again is that He might be our Lord, and that we might be His willing subjects, gladly rendering to Him the devotion of our grateful hearts. His Lordship continues even in death, when our bodies lie in the grave and our spirits and souls are in His presence.

14:10 Because this is true, it is folly for an overscrupulous Jewish Christian to condemn the brother who doesn't keep the Jewish calendar and who doesn't limit himself to kosher foods. Likewise, it is wrong for the strong brother to show contempt to the weak brother. The fact is that every one of us is going to stand before the judgment seat of God, and that will be the only evaluation that really counts.

Many manuscripts here speak of the judgment seat of *God* rather than of *Christ*. But we know that Christ will be the Judge, since the Father has committed all judgment to Him (John 5:22).

This judgment has to do with a believer's service, not his sins (1 Corinthians 3:11-15). It is a time of review and reward, and is not to be confused with the judgment of the Gentile nations (Matthew 25:31-46) or the judgment of the Great White Throne (Revelation 20:11-15). The latter is the final judgment of all the wicked dead.

14:11 The certainty of our appearance before the *bema* of God is reinforced by a quotation from Isaiah 45:23, where Jehovah Himself makes a strong affirmation that everyone will bow before Him in acknowledgment of His supreme authority.

14:12 And so it is clear that we will all give an account of *ourselves*, not of our brothers, to God. We judge one another too much, and without the proper authority or knowledge.

14:13 Instead of sitting in judgment on our fellow Christians in these matters of moral indifference, we should make the legitimate judicial decision that we will never do anything to hinder a brother in his spiritual progress. None of these nonessential matters is important enough for us to cause a brother to stumble or to fall.

14:14 Paul knew, and we know, that no foods are ceremonially unclean any longer, as they were for a Jew living under the law. Jesus pronounced all foods clean (Mark 7:19 NASB). The food we eat is sanctified by the Word of God and prayer (1 Timothy

4:5). It is sanctified by the Word in the sense that the Bible distinctly sets it apart as being good. It is sanctified by prayer when we ask God to bless it for His glory and for the strengthening of our bodies in His service.

But if a weak brother thinks it is wrong for him to eat pork, for example, then it is wrong. To eat it would be to violate his God-given conscience.

When Paul says here that nothing is unclean of itself, we must realize that he is speaking only of these indifferent matters. There are plenty of things in life that are unclean, such as pornographic literature, suggestive jokes, filthy movies, and every form of immorality. Paul's statement must be understood in the light of the context. The Christian does not contact ceremonial defilement by eating foods which the law of Moses branded as unclean.

14:15 When I sit down to eat with a weak brother, should I insist on my legitimate right to eat Crab Louis or Lobster Thermidor, even if I know he thinks it is wrong? If I do, I am not acting in love, because love thinks of others, not of self. Love foregoes its legitimate rights in order to promote the welfare of a brother.

A dish of food isn't as important as the spiritual well-being of a person for whom Christ died. And yet if I selfishly parade my rights in these matters, I can do irreparable damage in the life of a weak brother. It isn't worth it when you remember that his soul was redeemed at such a towering cost—the precious blood of Christ.

14:16 So the principle here is that we should not allow these secondary things, which are perfectly permissible in themselves, to give occasion to others to condemn us for our "looseness" or "lovelessness." It would be like sacrificing our good name for a mess of pottage.

14:17 What really counts in the Kingdom of God is not dietary regulations but spiritual realities.

The kingdom of God is the sphere where God is acknowledged as Supreme Ruler. In its widest sense, it includes all who even profess allegiance to God. But in its inward reality it includes only those who are born again. That is its usage here.

The subjects of the kingdom are not intended to be food faddists, gourmets, or wine connoisseurs. They should be characterized by lives of practical righteousness, by dispositions of peace and harmony, and by mind-sets of joy in the Holy Spirit.

14:18 It isn't what a man eats or doesn't eat that matters. It is a holy life that wins God's honor and man's approval. Those who put the emphasis on righteousness, peace, and joy serve Christ by obeying His teachings.

14:19 Thus another principle emerges. Instead of bickering over inconsequential matters, we should make every effort to maintain peace and harmony in the Christian fellowship. Instead of stumbling others by insisting on our rights, we should strive to build up others in their most holy faith.

14:20 God is doing a work in the life of each one of His children. It is frightening to think of hindering that work in the life of a weak brother over such secondary matters as foods, drinks, or days.

For the child of God, all foods are now clean. But it would be wrong for him to eat any specific food if, in doing so, he would offend a brother or stumble him in his Christian walk.

14:21 It is a thousand times better to refrain from meat or wine or anything else than to offend a brother or cause him to decline spiritually. Giving up our legitimate rights is a small price to pay for the care of one who is weak.

14:22 I may have complete liberty to partake of every kind of food, knowing that God gave it to be received with thanksgiving. But I should not needlessly flaunt that liberty before those who are weak. It is better to exercise that liberty in private, when no one could possibly be offended.

It is good to walk in the full enjoyment of one's Christian liberty, not being fettered by unwarranted scruples. But it is better to forego one's legitimate rights than have to condemn oneself for offending others. The man who avoids stumbling others is the happy man.

14:23 As far as the weak brother is concerned, it is wrong for him to eat anything about which he has conscientious scruples. His eating is not an act of faith; that is, he has a bad conscience about it. And it is a sin to violate one's conscience.

It is true that man's conscience is not always an infallible guide; it must be educated by the Word of God. But "Paul lays down the law that a man should follow his conscience, even though it be weak; otherwise moral personality would be destroyed."[1]

CHAPTER 15

15:1 The first 13 verses of this chapter continue the subject of the previous chapter, dealing with matters of moral indifference. Tensions had arisen between converts from Judaism and those from paganism, so Paul here pleads for harmonious relations between these Jewish and Gentile Christians.

Those who are strong (that is, with full liberty regarding things that are morally indifferent) should not please themselves by selfishly asserting their rights. Rather, they should treat their weak brothers with kindness and consideration, making full allowance for their excessive scruples.

15:2 Here the principle is this: don't live to please self. Live to please others, to do good to them, to build them up. This is the Christian approach.

15:3 The Savior has given us the example. He lived to please His Father, not Himself. He said, ''The reproaches of them that reproached Thee fell on me'' (Psalm 69:9). This means that He was so completely taken up with God's honor that when men insulted God He took it as a personal insult to Himself.

15:4 This quotation from the Psalms reminds us that the Old Testament Scriptures were written for our instruction. While they were not written directly *to* us, they contain invaluable lessons *for* us. As we encounter problems, conflicts, tribulations, and troubles, the Scriptures teach us to be steadfast and they impart comfort. Thus, instead of sinking under the waves, we are sustained by the hope that the Lord will see us through.

15:5 This consideration leads Paul to express the wish that the God who gives steadfastness and comfort will enable the strong and the weak, Gentile and Jewish Christians, to live harmoniously according to the teaching and example of Christ Jesus.

15:6 The result will be that the saints will be united in the worship of the God and Father of our Lord Jesus Christ. What a picture! Saved Jews and saved Gentiles worshiping the Lord with one mouth!

There are four mentions of the mouth in this epistle, forming a biographical outline of a well-saved soul. At the beginning, his mouth was full of cursing and bitterness (3:14). Then his mouth was stopped and he was brought in guilty before the Judge (3:19). Next he confesses with his mouth Jesus as Lord (10:9). And finally his mouth is actively praising and worshiping the Lord (15:6).

15:7 One more principle emerges from all this. In spite of any differences that might exist concerning secondary matters, we should receive one another as Christ received us. Here is the true basis for reception in the local assembly. We do not receive on the basis of denominational affiliation, or spiritual maturity, or social status. We should receive those whom Christ has received, in order to promote the glory of God.

15:8 In the next six verses the apostle reminds his readers that the ministry of the Lord Jesus includes Jews and Gentiles, and the implication is that our hearts should also be big enough to include both.

Certainly Christ came to serve the circumcision—that is, the Jewish people. God had repeatedly promised that He would send the Messiah to Israel, and Christ's coming confirmed the truth of those promises.

15:9 But Christ brings blessings to the Gentiles also. God purposed that the nations should hear the gospel, and that those people who believe should praise Him for His great mercy. This should not come as a surprise to Jewish believers, because it is frequently foretold in their Scriptures. In Psalm 18:49, for example, David anticipates the day when the Messiah will sing praise to God in the midst of a host of Gentile believers.

15:10 In Deuteronomy 32:43 the Gentiles are pictured as rejoicing in the blessings of salvation with the people of Israel.

15:11 In Psalm 117:1 we hear Israel calling on the Gentiles to worship Jehovah in the millennial reign of the Messiah.

15:12 Finally Isaiah adds his testimony to the inclusion of the Gentiles in the dominion of the Messiah (Isaiah 11:1,10). The particular point here is that the Gentiles would share in the privileges of the Messiah and of His gospel.

The Lord Jesus is the root of Jesse in the sense that He is Jesse's Creator, not that He sprang from Jesse (though that also is true). In Revelation 22:16 Jesus speaks of Himself as the root and offspring of David. As to His deity, He is David's Creator; as to His humanity, He is David's descendant.

15:13 So Paul closes this section with a gracious benediction, praying that the God who gives good hope through grace will fill the saints with joy and peace as they believe on Him. Perhaps he is thinking especially of Gentile believers here, as The Living Bible suggests, but the prayer is suitable for all. And it is true that those who abound in hope through the power of the Holy Spirit have no time to quarrel over nonessentials. Our common hope is a powerful unifying force in the Christian life.

15:14 In the rest of the chapter the apostle states his reason for writing to the Romans and his great desire to visit them.

Though he has never met the Roman Christians, he is confident that they will welcome his admonitions. This confidence is based on what he has heard of their goodness. In addition, he is assured of their knowledge of Christian doctrine, which qualifies them to admonish others.

15:15 In spite of his confidence in their spiritual progress, and in spite of the fact that he was a stranger to them, Paul didn't hesitate to remind them of some of their privileges and responsibilities. His frankness in writing as he did arose from the grace that God had given to him—that is, the grace that appointed him as an apostle.

15:16 He was appointed by God to be a sort of serving-priest of Christ Jesus to the Gentiles. He looked upon his work of ministering the gospel of God as a priestly function in which he presented saved Gentiles as an acceptable offering to God because they had been set apart by the Holy Spirit unto God through the new birth.

"What a radiant light this sheds on all our evangelistic and pastoral effort! Every soul won by the preaching of the gospel is not only brought into a place of safety and of blessing; he is an offering to God, a gift which gives Him satisfaction, the very offering He is seeking. Every soul carefully and patiently instructed in the things of Christ, and so made conformable to His likeness, is a soul in whom the Father takes pleasure. Thus we labor, not only for the saving of men, but for the satisfying of the heart of God. This is the most powerful motive."[1]

15:17 If Paul engages in boasting, it is not in his own person that he boasts, but in Christ Jesus. And it is not in his own accomplishments but in what God has been pleased to do through him. A humble servant of Christ does not engage in unseemly boasting, but yet he is conscious of the fact that God is using him to accomplish His purposes. Any temptation to pride is tempered by the realization that he is nothing in himself, that he has nothing except what he has received, and that he can do nothing for Christ except by the power of the Holy Spirit.

15:18 Paul does not presume to speak of what God had done through the ministry of others. He confines himself to the way the Lord had used *him* to win the Gentiles to obedience, both by what he said and by what he did—that is, by the message he preached and by the miracles he performed.

15:19 The Lord confirmed the apostle's message by miracles that taught spiritual lessons and that inspired amazement, and by various manifestations of the Spirit's power. The result was that he had fully preached the gospel, beginning at Jerusalem and extending in a circle to Illyricum (north of Macedonia, on the Adriatic Sea). The expression "from Jerusalem . . . unto Illyricum" describes the *geographical* extent of his ministry and not the chronological order.

15:20 In following this route, Paul's aim was to preach the gospel in virgin territory. His audiences were composed primarily of Gentiles who had never heard of Christ before. Thus he was not building on anyone else's foundation. Paul's example in pioneering in new areas does not necessarily bind other servants of the Lord to this exact activity. Some are called to move in and teach, for example, after new assemblies have been planted.

15:21 This foundational work among the Gentiles was a fulfillment of Isaiah's prophecy (52:15) that the Gentiles who had never previously been evangelized would see, and that those who had never previously heard the good news would understand and respond in true faith.

15:22 In his desire to plow untilled territory, Paul had been too occupied to get to Rome in the past.

15:23 Now, however, the foundation had been laid in the region described in 15:19. Others could build on the foundation. Paul was therefore free to fulfill his long-standing desire to visit Rome.

15:24 His plan was to stop off at Rome en route to Spain. He would not be able to stay long enough to enjoy all the fellowship with them that he would like, but his desire to enjoy their company would be partially satisfied at least. Then he knew that they would give whatever help was needed to complete his trip to Spain.

15:25 But in the meantime he had to go to Jerusalem to deliver the funds which had been collected among Gentile assemblies for the needy saints in Judea. This is the collection that we read about in 1 Corinthians 16:1 and 2 Corinthians 8 and 9.

15:26 The believers in Macedonia and Achaia had gladly contributed to a fund to relieve the distress among the poor Christians.

15:27 This collection was completely voluntary on the part of the donors, and also quite appropriate for them to give. After all, they had benefited spiritually by the coming of the gospel to them through Jewish believers. So it was not too much to expect that they would share with their Jewish brethren in a financial way.

15:28 As soon as Paul had accomplished this mission, delivering the funds as promised, he would visit Rome on his way to Spain.

15:29 He had every confidence that his visit to Rome would be accompanied by the full blessing which Christ always pours out when God's Word is preached in the power of the Holy Spirit.

The King James Version reads "the fulness of the blessing of the gospel of Christ," but the words "of the gospel" should be omitted, as in most modern versions. Paul was not coming to them with the gospel but with teaching for those who were already Christians.

15:30 The apostle closes this section with a fervent appeal for prayer. The basis on which he appeals is their mutual union with the Lord Jesus Christ and their love which came from the Holy Spirit.

He asks them to agonize in prayer to God for him. As Lenski says, "This calls for prayers into which one puts his whole heart and soul as do the contestants in the arena."[2]

15:31 Four specific prayer requests are given. First, the apostle asks for prayer that he will be protected from zealots in Judea who were fanatically opposed to the gospel, just as he himself had once been.

Second, he wants the Romans to pray that the Jewish saints will accept the relief funds in good grace. Strong religious prejudices remained against Gentile believers and against those who preached to the Gentiles. Then there is always the possibility of people being offended at the idea of receiving "charity." It often takes more grace to be on the receiving end than on the giving end.

15:32 The third request was that the Lord might see fit to make the visit to Rome a joyful one. The words "by the will of God" express Paul's desire to be led by the Lord in all things.

Last of all, he asks that his visit might be one in which he finds a measure of rest in the midst of a tumultuous and fatiguing ministry.

15:33 And now Paul closes the chapter with the prayer that the

God who is the source of peace might be their portion.

In this chapter the Lord has been named the God of patience and consolation (v. 5), the God of hope (v. 13), and now the God of peace. He is the source of everything good and of everything a poor sinner needs now and eternally.

CHAPTER 16

At first glance the closing chapter of Romans seems to be an uninteresting catalog of names that have little or no meaning for us today. However, upon closer study this neglected chapter yields many important lessons for the believer.

16:1 Phoebe is introduced as a servant or deaconess of the church in Cenchrea. We need not think of her as belonging to some special religious order. Any sister who serves in connection with a local assembly is a deaconess.

16:2 Whenever the early Christians traveled from one assembly to another, they carried letters of introduction. This was a real courtesy to the assembly being visited and a help to the visitor.

So the apostle here introduces Phoebe and asks that she be welcomed as a true believer in a manner worthy of fellow-believers. He further asks that she be assisted in every way possible. Her commendation is that she has given herself to the ministry of helping others, including Paul himself. Perhaps she was the tireless sister who was forever showing hospitality to preachers and other believers in Cenchrea.

16:3 Next Paul sends greetings to Priscilla and Aquila, who had been such valiant co-workers of his in the service of Christ Jesus. How we can thank God for Christian couples who pour themselves out in sacrificial labor for the cause of Christ!

16:4 On one occasion Priscilla and Aquila actually risked their lives for Paul—a heroic act of which no details are given. But the apostle is grateful, and so are the assemblies of converted Gentiles to whom he ministered.

16:5 ''Greet the church that is in their house.'' This means that an actual congregation of believers met in their home. Church buildings were unknown until the second century. Earlier, when Priscilla and Aquila lived in Corinth, they had an assembly in their house there also.

Epaenetus means ''praiseworthy.'' No doubt this first convert in the province of Asia (NASB), not Achaia (KJV), was true to his name. Paul speaks of him as ''my beloved.''

16:6 The prominence of women's names in this chapter emphasizes their wide sphere of usefulness (vv. 1,3,6,12, etc.). Mary worked like a trojan for the saints.

16:7 We do not know when Andronicus and Junia were prisoners with Paul. We cannot be sure whether the word *kinsman* means that they were close relatives of the apostle or simply fellow Jews. Again, we do not know whether the expression ''of note among the apostles'' means that they were respected by the apostles or that they themselves were outstanding apostles. All we can know for certain is that they became Christians before Paul.

16:8 Next we meet Amplias, beloved by the apostle. We would never have heard of many of these people except for their connection with Calvary. That is the only greatness about any of us.

16:9 Urbane wins the title ''fellow-worker'' and Stachys ''my beloved.'' Romans 16 is like a miniature of the Judgment Seat of Christ, where there will be praise for every instance of faithfulness to Christ.

16:10 Apelles had come through some great trial with flying colors and had won the seal of ''approved in Christ.''

Paul salutes the household of Aristobulus, probably meaning Christian slaves belonging to this grandson of Herod the great.

16:11 Herodion was probably a slave also. A kinsman of Paul, he may have been the only *Jewish* slave belonging to Aristobulus.

Then some of the slaves belonging to Narcissus were also believers, and Paul includes them in his greetings.

Even those who are lowest on the social ladder are not excluded from the choicest blessings of Christianity. The inclusion of slaves in this list of names is a lovely reminder that in Christ all social distinctions are obliterated because we are all one in Him.

16:12 Tryphena and Tryphosa had names that meant ''dainty'' and ''luxurious,'' but they were veritable workhorses in their service for the Lord.

The beloved Persis was another of those workers that are so needed in local churches but seldom appreciated until they are gone.

16:13 Rufus may be the son of Simon, who carried the cross for Jesus (Matthew 27:32). He was ''chosen in the Lord'' not only as to his salvation but also as to his Christian character; that is, he was a choice saint.

The mother of Rufus had shown maternal kindness to Paul, and this earned his affectionate title ''my mother.''

16:14 Perhaps Asyncritus, Phlegon, Hermas, Patrobas, and Hermes were active in a household church, like the one in the house of Priscilla and Aquila (16:3,5).

16:15 Philologus and Julia, Nereus and his sister, and Olympas may have been the nucleus of another household church.

16:16 The holy kiss was the common mode of affectionate greeting among the saints then and is still practiced in some countries today. It is designated as a *holy* kiss to guard against impropriety. In our culture, the kiss has been replaced by the handshake.

The churches in Achaia, where Paul was writing, joined in sending their greetings.

16:17 The apostle cannot close the letter without a warning against ungodly teachers who might worm their way into the assembly. The Christians should be on their guard against any such who form parties around themselves and set traps to destroy the faith of the unwary. They should be on the lookout for any whose teaching is contrary to the sound doctrine which the Christians had received, and should avoid them completely.

16:18 These false teachers are not obedient to our Lord Christ. They obey their own appetites. And they are all too successful in hoodwinking the unsuspecting by their winsome and flattering speech.

16:19 Paul rejoiced that his readers' obedience to the Lord was well-known. But still he wanted them to be able to discern and obey sound teaching and to be unresponsive to all that was evil.

16:20 In this way, the God who is the source of peace would give them a swift victory over Satan.

The apostle's characteristic benediction wishes all needed enablement for the saints as they journey toward glory.

16:21 We know Timothy, Paul's son in the faith and faithful co-worker. We know nothing of Lucius except that he, like Paul, was of Jewish parentage. We may have previously met Jason (Acts 17:5) and Sosipater (Acts 20:4), also Jews.

16:22 Tertius was the one to whom Paul had dictated the letter. He takes the liberty of adding his personal well-wishes to the readers.

16:23 There are at least four men by the name of Gaius mentioned in the New Testament. This is probably the same one spoken of in 1 Corinthians 1:14. He was noted for his hospitality, not only to Paul but to any Christians who needed it.

Erastus was treasurer of the city of Corinth, but was he the same person mentioned in Acts 19:22 and/or 2 Timothy 4:20? We cannot be sure. Quartus is mentioned simply as a brother, but after all, what an honor, what a dignity!

16:24 Most modern versions of the Bible omit this verse because the words are not found in the best manuscripts. An almost-identical benediction is found at the end of verse 20.

16:25 The epistle closes with a doxology. It is addressed to the God who is able to make His people stand firm in accordance with the gospel which Paul preached and which he calls "my gospel." There is only one way of salvation, of course; but it was entrusted to him as the apostle to the Gentiles, whereas Peter, for example, preached it to the Jews. It is, in short, the public heralding of the message concerning Jesus Christ.

And it is concerned with the revelation of a marvelous truth which had been kept hidden since the world began.

A mystery, in the New Testament, is a truth never previously known, and a truth which human intellect could never discover, but one which has now been made known.

16:26 The particular mystery spoken of here is the truth that believing Jews and believing Gentiles are made fellow-heirs, fellow-members of the Body of Christ, and fellow-partakers of his promise in Christ by the gospel (Ephesians 3:6).

It has now been made manifest by the writing of the prophets—not the prophets of the Old Testament but those of the New Testament period. It was unknown in the Old Testament Scriptures but has been revealed in the prophetic writings of the New Testament (see Ephesians 2:20; 3:5).

It is the gospel message which God has commanded to be made known to all the nations in order that men might obey the message and be saved.

16:27 God alone is the source and display of pure wisdom, and to Him belongs glory, through Jesus Christ our Mediator, forever.

And so ends Paul's magnificent epistle. How indebted we are to the Lord for it! And how poor we would be without it!

NOTES

Chapter 1
1. F. W. H. Myers, *St. Paul* (poem).
2. *Daily Notes of the Scripture Union* (further documentation unavailable).

Chapter 2
1. A. P. Gibbs, *Preach and Teach the Word*, p. 12/4.
2. L. S. Chafer, *Systematic Theology, Vol. III*, p. 376.

Chapter 3
1. A. T. Pierson, *Shall We Continue in Sin?* (pagination unavailable).
2. *Our Daily Bread*, article by Paul Van Gorder.

Chapter 4
1. *Daily Notes of the Scripture Union* (further documentation unavailable).
2. C. H. Mackintosh, *The Mackintosh Treasury*, p. 66.

Chapter 5
1. Joseph Dillow, *Speaking in Tongues*, p. 51.

Chapter 6
1. J. Oswald Sanders, *Spiritual Problems*, p. 112.
2. Ruth Paxson, *The Wealth, Walk, and Warfare of the Christian*, p. 108.

3. C. E. Macartney, *Macartney's Illustrations,* pp. 378,379.
4. James Denney (further documentation unavailable).
5. Charles Gahan (further documentation unavailable).
6. Marcus Rainsford, *Lectures on Romans VI,* p. 172.
7. A. T. Pierson, *Shall We Continue in Sin?* p. 45.

Chapter 7
1. Harry Foster, article in *Toward the Mark,* p. 110.
2. George Cutting (further documentation unavailable).

Chapter 8
1. C. H. Mackintosh (further documentation unavailable).

Chapter 9
1. *New Scofield Reference Bible,* p. 1317.
2. G. Campbell Morgan, *Searchlights from the Word,* pp. 335, 336.
3. Albert Barnes, *Barnes' Notes on the New Testament,* p. 617.
4. C. R. Erdman, *The Epistle of Paul to the Romans,* p. 109.

Chapter 10
1. William Kelly, *Notes on the Epistle to the Romans,* p. 206.
2. James Denney, quoted by Kenneth Wuest in *Romans in the Greek New Testament,* p. 178.
3. Charles Hodge, *The Epistle to the Romans,* p. 545.

Chapter 11
1. George Williams, *The Student's Commentary on the Holy Scriptures,* p. 871.
2. A. W. Pink, *The Attributes of God,* p. 13.

Chapter 12
1. Norman Grubb, *C. T. Studd, Cricketer and Pioneer,* p. 141.
2. Isaac Watts, "When I Survey the Wondrous Cross" (hymn).
3. Charles Hodge, *The Epistle to the Romans,* p. 613.
4. A. H. Strong, *Systematic Theology,* p. 712.

5. R. C. H. Lenski, *St. Paul's Epistle to the Romans,* p. 780.
6. J. N. Darby, from footnote on Romans 12:21 in his *New Translation.*
7. George Washington Carver (further documentation unavailable).

Chapter 14
1. Merrill Unger, *Unger's Bible Dictionary,* p. 219.

Chapter 15
1. G. Campbell Morgan, *Searchlights from the Word,* p. 337.
2. R. C. H. Lenski, *St. Paul's Epistle to the Romans,* p. 895.

BIBLIOGRAPHY

BOOKS REFERRED TO OR QUOTED IN THE TEXT.

Barnes, Albert. *Barnes' Notes on the New Testament*. Grand Rapids: Kregel Publications, 1975.

Chafer, Lewis Sperry. *Systematic Theology, Vol. III*. Dallas: Dallas Seminary Press, 1948.

Dillow, Joseph. *Speaking in Tongues*. Grand Rapids: Zondervan Publishing House, 1976.

Erdman, C. R. *The Epistle of Paul to the Romans*. Philadelphia: The Westminster Press, 1925.

Gibbs, A. P. *Preach and Teach the Word*. Oak Park, Illinois: Emmaus Bible School, 1971.

Grubb, Norman P. *C. T. Studd, Cricketer and Pioneer*. London: Lutterworth Press, 1957.

Hodge, Charles. *The Epistle to the Romans*. New York: George H. Doran Company, 1882.

Kelly, William. *Notes on the Epistle to the Romans*. London: G. Morrish, 1873.

Lenski, R. C. H. *St. Paul's Epistle to the Romans*. Minneapolis: Augsburg Publishing House, 1961.

Macartney, Clarence Edward. *Macartney's Illustrations*. New York: Abingdon Press, 1946.

Mackintosh, C. H. *The Mackintosh Treasury*. Neptune, New Jersey: Loizeaux Bros., 1976.

Morgan, G. Campbell. *Searchlights from the Word*. London: Oliphants, 1970.

Myers, F. W. H. *St. Paul*. London: Samuel Bagster & Sons Ltd., n.d.

Paxson, Ruth. *The Wealth, Walk, and Warfare of the Christian*. London: Oliphants, 1944.

Pierson, A. T. *Shall We Continue in Sin?* New York: Gospel Publishing, n.d.

Pink, Arthur W. *The Attributes of God*. Swengel, Pennsylvania: Bible Truth Depot, n.d.

Rainsford, Marcus. *Lectures on Romans VI*. London: Charles J. Thynne, 1898.

Sanders, J. Oswald. *Spiritual Problems*. Chicago: Moody Press, 1971.

Strong, A. H. *Systematic Theology*. Philadelphia: The Judson Press, 1943.

Unger, Merrill. *Unger's Bible Dictionary*. Chicago: Moody Press, 1966.

Williams, George. *The Student's Commentary on the Holy Scriptures*. Grand Rapids: Kregel Publications, 1953.

Wuest, Kenneth S. *Romans in the Greek New Testament*. Grand Rapids: Wm. B. Eerdmans Publishing Company, 1964.

ARTICLES AND PERIODICALS

Daily Notes of the Scripture Union. London: C.S.S.M., various dates.

Our Daily Bread. Grand Rapids: Radio Bible Class.

Toward the Mark. Weston-super-Mare, Vol. 5, No. 6 (1976).

BIBLE VERSIONS

American Standard Version (ASV)
English Revised Version (ERV)
The Living Bible, Paraphrased (TLB)
New American Standard Bible (NASB)
New English Bible (NEB)
New International Version (NIV)

New Scofield Reference Bible
New Testament in Modern English by J. B. Phillips
New Translation by J. N. Darby
A New Translation of the Bible by James Moffatt
Revised Standard Version (RSV)